Triple Your Business This Year

Dr. Bruce Parker

Triple Your Business This Year

Dr. Bruce Parker

Text copyright © 2014 Dr Bruce Parker

All Rights Reserved

TABLE OF CONTENTS

Introduction

Chapter 1: Common Mistakes Business People Make In Their Marketing Efforts

Chapter 2: Where Did Clichés Come From?

Chapter 3: The Sales funnel

Chapter 4: Innovation

Chapter 5: Strategic Messaging Formula

Chapter 6: Modern Neuroscience

Chapter 7: Capture

Chapter 8: Hot Buttons

Chapter 9: Connect

Chapter 10: Inform

Chapter 11: Incentivize

Chapter 12: Automate

Chapter 13: Internet Suite

Chapter 14: Systematized Sales Process

Bonus Section: The 5 step Process to Acquire New Clients

Chapter 15: An Example of the System Working

Chapter 16: Summary

Introduction

The first thing you must know is... *There is enough money in your industry and your market for you to double or triple your sales and revenue in the next year alone*. The money and the sales are just sitting there right now waiting for you to come and get them. The problem and the reason why you're not making those sales right now is because you're doing you're marketing and advertising all wrong and I'm going to prove it to you.

Hi, this is Dr Bruce Parker and I'm the president of Local Market Fusion. In this book I'm going to reveal a complete marketing system that when executed properly will cause your prospects and customers to realize that you're the only company in your industry they should be doing business with.

In fact I will show you exactly how you can make the advantages of doing business with your company so obvious to your prospects and customers that they quickly and easily draw this conclusion; *"I'd have to be completely insane to work with anyone else but you no matter the price."*

My role as Business and Marketing Consultant

I am a doctor of Chiropractic who with an entrepreneurial spirit expanded my first primary clinic, to ultimately develop and operate 13 clinics. Then began a career of consulting to 100's of chiropractors on how to expand their clinics, as well as become the president of the professional corporation of a chain of 18 clinics that were preparing for a public offering.

My expertise as I see it was developing a sales funnel within the practice to acquire, connect and transform potential patients into long term clients. Marketing for new clients is extremely necessary, my attitude was always on retaining those clients I fought so hard to acquire.

The Cold market is people in your community that don't really know or trust you, and they are harder to get a buying decision from today than ever, especially in this post 2007 economy.

My focus still remains to provide internal marketing so as to turn cold market suspects into long term raving fans, demonstrating their love for our service by the referral of friends and families. Yet to develop long term raving fans you must learn to attract those that do not love or trust you and convert those people into the raving fans… therefor this book is focused on marketing a small business or professional practice in today's more skeptical marketplace.

The goal of this book is to teach you the proven system I have developed to dominate your local market and align your business / practice as the market leader in your niche or industry… The goal I have for you is for your prospects to say in their minds… *"I'd have to be completely insane to work with anyone else but you no matter the price."*

My career experience was totally pioneered, fueled by a vision to propagate a message that ever person on this planet could live with optimal health. I knew no one who had operated multiple clinics, so this experience gave my multiple opportunities to make multiple mistakes and make multiple discoveries, as well when it came to, marketing a practice, managing a TEAM, as well as managing the business and patient care.

So given that back ground, my terminology may slip form referring to a practice or a business. This is not a point of confusion it is a point of clarification. I see a law practice, dentist office, chiropractic office, acupuncture clinic or med spa as a practice, since they are engaged in selling and providing a service, yet they are a business and need to be managed as a business.

My consulting has been primarily as a chiropractic consultant, yet I have been asked to help others in business as well; I have consulted to a skateboard manufacturer, an electronics contractor a dentist, acupuncturist, retail store, and an investment group poised to create a chain of Chiropractic offices for a public offering.

What I have discovered is no matter the product or service each business required a sales funnel, a clearly planned annual marketing plan as well as credibility documents and branding a "culture" for the use of the product or service.

All businesses require a marketing plan that has the long term value of a customer in mind with a strategic plan that will clearly give a return on investment (ROI). The business needs to be operated with the understanding that marketing is internal as well as external and is not an option to be performed when business is down. Marketing is a constant and there are choices and strategies to choose from as to what marketing you deliver, there is internal marketing and external and they must remain consistent by following a strategic and consistent marketing plan.

I have also noticed that in many of the industries a "Me too" business plan is propagated throughout the industry. As in the case of the Chiropractic profession certain business practices have become traditions. Practices are built as to a certain financial plan, with policies restricting or omitting the use of cash or insurance, with a fee structure that changes with the decision to use cash or insurance for reimbursement of a same or similar service. These offices also serve all... from a welfare recipient to an industrial or auto accident victim, as well as a family looking for general health care, and the well intentioned doctors attempt to make their financial policies fit all needs which become a major source of stress for them.

Promoting the practice also has its practice of, "me too" promotions, with cliché advertising; with the chronic use of: Asking their friends what is working for you... with no real strategic market planning.

There are also traditions in the business plans to operate a practice, that are not good for today's economic climate yet prevail because it was "what we did back in '42". It is necessary for all business to have a clear business plan with a financial strategy that works in today's economy, which promotes efficiency and TEAM accountability.

In writing this book February of 2014, our country is just emerging from a devastating recession that was called by some, a depression as bad as the one in 1929, stating the 2007-2009 recession, was the most severe economic downturn since the Great Depression.

Many leaders that have as their focus of living with a Positive Mental Attitude denied the 2007-9 recession even existed and any real damage was done because of the thinking of the nay-sayers. Yet looking at the economic situations that are have transpired the recession in this authors opinion was real and because of the recession I have observed that we are in an emerging new economy, yet I still observe business people promoting fees and prices at pre-recession prices, and as insurance reimbursement for health care is dwindling out of existence and becoming under government control, I still observe practitioners charging high fees once reimbursed by yet no longer by insurance, yet not affordable for those without insurance; rather than becoming creative for today's economic environment.

Many of the rules of business have changed, and while many focus on what is no longer working, the smart money is moving towards developing their businesses with the new economy in mind. This goes for marketing and business strategies as well; which is the purpose of this book.

The system I'm going to share with you is called the Local Market Domination Program and it is unique in our industry because of its comprehensive nature; it's not about running ads or using new technological techniques, in fact I am quite certain you have never heard anything like this before.

You will find that the Local Market Domination Program covers basically everything that is necessary to ensure that your company becomes number one in your industry.

When I say number one I mean number one! The purpose of this marketing system is not just to help you acquire a few new customers; if your goal is to learn a tip of two about some simple new little marketing gimmick, or a cool direct mail idea, or a new internet marketing trick, or a way to get found online, or a new graphic or design idea, or anything like that then this is not the program for you. Sure I'll cover some of those ideas briefly since our program is comprehensive, but that's not the focus of what we're going to learn here.

In this book you're going to learn everything you need to know so that you can rise to a place of total dominance. We're not talking about increasing revenue a little here and a little there; we're talking total dominance in your niche.

I want to show you how you can become the 900 pound Gorilla in your industry and in your market and receive all the benefits that come with being number one. In this program I will teach you the problems with your existing marketing and advertising, and the neural and psychological basis for effective marketing techniques, as the only way to achieve market domination and the immediate solutions you can begin implementing tomorrow to set you on course for "Local Market Dominance".

In fact I'm even going to make you a guarantee and here it is; after reading to this book if you do not feel like you've learned anything valuable enough to earn back triple the amount of money you invested in the book, I will give you 100% of your money back, so there's simply no risk involved; you can't lose.

Now because I personally hate to have my time wasted, I am going to assume you are the same, so I'm going to get right into the content and get to the good stuff... OK?

So let's get started.

Chapter 1:
Common Mistakes Business People Make In Their Marketing Efforts

Now before we can really get started and explain to you the details of the five steps in the Local Market Domination Program I need to share with you the two most common marketing mistakes that nearly all businesses owners make. If you've done any advertising or marketing for your business ever, at all; I can virtually guarantee that you've been making at least one of the following two common marketing mistakes. It doesn't matter if you've been doing business with 5, 10, even 20 years or more! Even those who are getting what most people would consider pretty good results; I'm here to tell you that these two mistakes have cost you a lot of money in lost opportunity and lost business.

I'm not just blowing a bunch of smoke here to catch your attention; in fact I want you to go get a few examples of your marketing material right now. Get a brochure, radio scripts, TV ad, newspaper or magazine ad, your website; whatever it is, get a copy or access to it right now so you can evaluate it for yourself as I describe these two mistakes. I want you to objectively judge your own marketing and advertising and make a determination for yourself whether or not what I'm saying has value.

Let's begin with mistake number one; using one of the three forbidden phrases. The phrases that use clichés; In marketing... clichés are essentially the kiss of death; let me give you the definition of the cliché as pertains to marketing. Clichés are words or phrases that are dull, obvious or predictable; that lack power to create interest because they're overused and unoriginal; that are nevertheless still commonly used as though they were unique or distinctive. let me give you some examples of clichés, they're words and phrases like; "highest quality", "best service", "largest selection", "gets the job done right the first time", "30 years of experience", "in business since 1987", "honest hard-working", "you tried the rest now try the best", "number one", "your dealer of choice", "state-of-the-art"; blah-blah- blah-blah.

Does this sound familiar? Of course it does, you've heard this kind of junk for years but now here's the killer question; do you have these terms in your marketing? I bet you do. I don't even know you but if I was a betting man, I'd bet the farm on the fact that your advertising and marketing is loaded with clichés.

Right now take a look for yourself. Here's the deal these clichés which fill up your marketing and advertising are killing your profits and destroying your marketing opportunities, these clichés don't distinguish from or separate you in the marketplace, they don't quantify or specify anything, they're not believable, they're usually not provable and they cause your prospects to minimise, discount, disbelieve or worse of all ignore you altogether. Ultimately your target market ends up believing that you and your business is just like everybody else in your industry; this is why your target market always ends up grinding you on price, regardless of how great you claim your service is or how much better you think you are than your competitors.

None of that matters because you introduce yourself to the marketplace as one more scoop of vanilla in a whole sea of vanilla; and I'm not saying that there's anything wrong with vanilla, but what I am saying is that if you're perceived as being vanilla just like everybody else, The only real message you're portraying to your target market is; me too.

Think about how pitiful that is, this is why you're not dominating your market and this is why your sales and revenues are dependent upon the immediate needs of the market, not your ability to win over more and more customers and dominate your sector. That's a big difference.

Let me break this down further for you by using some objective evaluations so you can determine if you really are using clichés in your advertising. Let's review these three evaluations which expose what we call the three forbidden phrases.

Cliché evaluation number one is called; well I would hope so.

Seriously that's the name of the evaluation and here's the deal. Look at the statements and phrases in your advertising and then ask yourself this question, could or would my prospects immediately respond to these statements with; well I would hope so.

For example; I'm looking right now at a couple of ads for a Chiropractor. This one says; we care about our patients! Well I would hope so you're a Chiropractor, you better care! How about this one: Chiropractor now accepting new patients. Well I would hope so, isn't that why you are promoting your practice? I can't believe it; this Chiropractor here says "painless care"; maybe I should call this one quick... Instead of one of the other 500 Chiropractors in town who also say they are painless as well.

It is so painfully obvious that it is ridiculous. Or how about this common statement that says: tender loving care, well I would hope so, what else would you expect them to say. Hey we're lousy, will hurt you and make you worse?

Of course not; everybody is going to say great things about themselves if they can get away with it. Do you see how ridiculous these statements are, yet everyone uses them including you. The biggest problem here is the fact that you're true uniqueness and your true strengths; the real benefits that your customers get when they do business with you over your competitors will never shine when you use clichés too.

Take a look at your advertising especially all your printed advertising and marketing materials did they pass the; *"well I would hope so evaluation"* or are they full of clichés. If you're using clichés then you need to make changes or at least you'd better hope and pray that one of your competitors doesn't get a hold of this book. This is only evaluation number one; let's go to the other two evaluations.

Cliché evaluation number two:

Pay close attention to this one because the question is not who else can do what you do but who else can say what you say; the answer is usually anyone and everyone. Here is a painter who says that he is California's best, really who else can say that. Now this guy might actually be the best in California or the best in the entire universe as far as I'm concerned but do you actually believe it just because he said it.

Who else can say that? Can't the guy on the next page of the phone book where I got this ad, who says where integrity and quality meet can't he also says that he is California's best; of course he can.

See these statements are dull and obvious; they lack power to create interest because they're overused and unoriginal and you know what; they were nevertheless used as though they were unique or distinctive. Now look at you ad, read a few lines and then ask yourself this who else can say that? If one of your competitors can say it then you failed this evaluation.

Now one of the most common clichés in advertising is to tell us how long you've been in business; everybody thinks that matters but I promise you it doesn't. Here's an illustration I'm looking at a website for a chiropractor who thinks you should visit his practice because he's been a chiropractor for over 29 years... well who else can say that? How about his competitor who has the next listing on Google who was been serving for over 30 years; see what I mean. In fact I want you to go online right now and type in any local industry to see what you find on companies websites.

Look up attorneys, mechanic's, financial advisers, banks, contractors, designers, manufacturers, architects, technology companies, software companies or any industry imaginable and compare them to their competitors who were also on the first page of Google; and see what you find. What you're going to find is that everybody is using virtually identical marketing statements they're all clichés. Everybody is saying what everybody else is saying; meaning that the marketplace has to assume that everybody is basically the same. Therefore the only thing that should matter is price; well do you hate getting grinded on price? Well now you know why; it's because you've become a commodity by way of your own promotions over the years.

So let's move on to the third evaluation which often hurts the most because with this one it all becomes very apparent that folks have a marketing problem. **Cliché evaluation number three is called the cross out write in test**. For this evaluation I'm going to have you cross out the name of your company in your advertisement and then write in the name of your competitor; cross out write in, get it.

Now tell me this, is the ad still valid? If so you just failed the test. Another way to illustrate this is to do it in reverse; cross out your competitors name and replace it with your company's name, now tell me is the ad still valid? I mean really I don't care if you absolutely know that you have higher quality than your competitor because your competitor can still say that they have higher quality than you; even if it's not true.

I can give you hundreds of other examples for insurance companies who can give you fast easy quotes or dentists who offer complete dental care or landscape contractors who cut to perfection; but the bottom line is that none of these ads have passed the cross out write in test or the other commonplace evaluations.

Now when we implement the Local Market Domination program into your business one of the first things we do is remove all of the clichés from your existing advertising, we innovate your company and create specific and strategic marketing headlines, messages and campaigns that absolutely separate you from your competitors and cause your prospects and customers to draw this simple conclusion. *I'd have to be completely insane to work with anybody else but you; no matter the price.* We even have a specific marketing evaluation form that we use to guarantee that you'll never put out dreadful ads with clichés that get lacklustre results again.

You see as I've already mentioned; clichés cause your marketplace to assume that you and your competitors are all the same but that's probably not true. You might have the best business of its kind in your industry and since your ads and your competitor's ads all use clichés then the marketplace can't tell who actually offers the best value, so they call you up and ask you the same question, that you're probably really sick of hearing which is; how much do you charge? Which is the question as your product or service becomes a commodity, stripped of its uniqueness and value.

Well, It doesn't have to be that way; let me give you one last example. Take a look at one of your company's brochures, what's on top of the front cover? More than likely you've put your company name and a logo there; well guess what, if you did you just failed the exam.

Let me explain why; nobody cares who you are until they know what you can do for them. Here's another secret; instead of putting your company name or logo on the front cover of your brochure you should put a hot button loaded headline that you make sure connects with your prospects and makes them beg to read the contents on the inside. I'll explain what I mean by this and exactly how to do it.

So is this making sense to you? Is this starting to become evident that using clichés might be a problem to you right now, and that you'd have tremendous competitive advantage if you could figure out how to fix it? Well we're going to review the local market domination formula for you a little bit later on in this book. I'm going to show you exactly how to fix it and to get rid of clichés forever. I'm going to teach you how to become a communications expert so you can start gaining the results from your marketing that you should be getting. So now let's move on to the second most common marketing mistake.

The second most common marketing mistake

The second most common marketing mistake that businesses make is what we call fragmented or piecemeal marketing. This is absolutely the wrong approach to marketing yet it is the most common approach in business today; everybody's doing it including you and your competitors. The good news or bad if you don't, is that the first one to fix this problem basically wins. Seriously!

Let me explain fragmented marketing which is the wrong way to do it in contrast to what we call systamatized marketing which is the right way to do it. Fragmented marketing means that there is no cohesive message or comprehensive system handling your marketing for you; instead when you buy marketing or advertising it is developed by the company creating the ad, right?

Think back to the last advertisement or marketing piece that you created for your company, what was it? A brochure, a website, a printed ad or radio spot; so now let me ask you a question, who created the final product for you? They did, didn't they?

The radio station created your radio spot, the magazine created your magazine ad, the design company created your brochure, the web design company created the website and the video production company developed the content for your video, right?

Think about how fragmented that makes your marketing efforts, all of those different companies have different ideas about what your marketing message should be based on their limited experience. Inevitably they all use clichés and then they try to throw in their own dose of creativity.

Think about how wrong this is, you need to develop your own message, you shouldn't leave it to others and you certainly shouldn't leave it to multiple teams of others who don't really have your best interests in mind nor do they care about your position in the market place.

This is why you need a marketing system in place, the system dictates the content of the advertisements and it dictates the sequence that your prospects go through and the message that your prospects hear as they're ultimately lead to your door.

A systamatized marketing program would actually facilitate the decision making process; in other words it would define what criteria your prospects should look for in a company, product or service and in doing so it would lead them to buy from you and not your competitor.

Here's another question to illustrate this problem; take a look at your last advertisement, I know it's filled with clichés but here's the question. How much money did you pay to have the content of that advertisement strategically created and formulated to ensure maximum results? I'm not talking about the design; I'm talking about the content, the message, what you actually said in the advertisement not what it looks like?

That's what I thought, you paid nothing right? 99.9% of the time you only pay to have the advertisement produced or designed or you pay for the spots or airtime. The content was usually just thrown together by the designer, the production team or the sales person. Think about it, the most important part of your marketing material that is the content and message was put together for free by people who usually have no idea how to create good messaging anyway.

Have you ever heard the saying, you get what you pay for? Well I hate to tell you this but if you've never paid anybody to create the actual message or content for your advertising campaigns then you got what you paid for.

So here's the point, when you think of marketing you need to start thinking about your message, you need to think about what you're going to say and how you're going to say it. When you think of marketing don't think of the media anymore, think of messaging. Only once you have the right message should you then start considering which media to run your marketing in.

This is the difference between a marketing system and typical fragmented marketing. A marketing system considers first the message then it develops the message and installs it in a comprehensive marketing system which facilitates the prospects decision making process.

Finally it chooses the best media to promote those messages so as to generate leads to pump into the system. Do you see how much more effective that is then typical fragmented marketing.

I am going to show you how you can use Local Market Domination program to build and develop your own complete marketing system so that you ultimately can achieve what we call comprehensive marketing synergy. I know it will probably be an a'ha moment for you, when you notice the light bulb going on.

Chapter 2: Where Did Clichés Come From?

After reading the few chapters, you might be asking yourself why are we all using clichés; it seems obvious that that is the wrong way to do it but everybody is doing it? While I don't want to spend too much time answering that question because I want to get to the solutions quickly for you; but the answer to this question is actually more important than you realize , and understanding the answer to this question is essential in order you to be able to fix the problem.

So have you ever seen the invisible gorilla experiments? If not let me explain it to you; the experiment was devised by Dan Symons who received his Ph.D. in experimental psychology from Cornell University, you can find the video on YouTube by typing in invisible gorilla into the search field.

In the video there are three students with white shirts and three students with black shirts; the white team passes a basketball to one another and the black team does the same but the catch is they're all moving around and walking in amongst one another; your job as the observer is to count how many times the white shirt pass the ball to one another, that's it.

The video only lasts about 20 seconds but here's where it gets funny; in the middle of the video a guy wearing a gorilla suit walks right into the video frame, stands right in front of camera, faces the camera, leans back, pounds his chest and then walks out of the camera frame. It's hilarious because he's right there in front of your face pounding his chest but guess what; most people watching the video never see a gorilla; I'm serious. I know it's hard to believe but it's true.

My personal experience has been that well over 80% of people I show it to never see the gorilla. In fact, I always hope that at least one person in the group sees the gorilla because if not my audience accuses me of showing two different videos. You know why; because humans simply cannot believe that a full-sized gorilla can walk right in front of their face, pound his chest and walk away without them ever knowing that it's true; it's unbelievably true.

This is just part of human nature and the reason why this happens is because the viewer is distracted counting basketball passes. You see, if the viewer was not given the task of counting basketball passes, basically 100% of all people would see the gorilla; but because people are distracted with another task they completely miss these incredibly obvious things happening right in front of them. This is the exact same way the street magicians and pickpockets operate they're called masters of misdirection because they've learned how to focus your attention on something else, while stealing your wallet, watch, your purse or producing a card from a card deck.

Think about how that applies to your work, you're pretty focused on running your business; I bet you are. I bet you're a very effective and focused business person who runs his business pretty efficiently or at least like to think about that as it pertains to marketing. If you're distracted by industry news reports, inventories, profit and loss to HR issues, turnover, insurance, sales forecast, personal problems and payroll and the other 273 other relevant issues that you need to pay attention too so that you can effectively run your business.

It's highly likely that some very obvious and important gorillas are pounding their chests in front of your face and you're missing them altogether. In fact the same goes for other areas of your life like your relationships, your family, your health, your faith and other important things. You should really consider that, but anyhow we have to talk about marketing right now and I want to help you understand where this invisible gorilla came from in marketing and advertising.

For the sake of this discussion an invisible gorilla represents the two common mistakes we just discussed; that is using clichés and using fragmented marketing. In order to understand this we need to take a quick trip down memory lane; let's go back to late 1800s. Back then advertising in America was done mostly on a local or regional level and because of that the advertising was very comparative and the competition was really fierce. Advertisers didn't use lame clichés; instead they were very specific about why I should buy from them and not their competitors.

This continued all the way through the middle of the 20th century but then the most significant change in the history of advertising came to America around 1945; it was then that television was first introduced commercially to America. By the time the 50s rolled around the typical American family had one television set, they only received three channels but here's the thing. People were enamoured with this new device and they basically sat around every night watching it; it was a powerful opportunity. Some of the biggest companies in the country saw the opportunity and jumped on it, they realize d that they could reach pretty much everybody in the whole country using the TV and they could do it pretty cheap. They could buy a TV commercial that almost reached everybody in the entire country for around $4000 a minute; it was the deal of the century even in 1950s money. So when this began to catch on, the price of the commercial skyrocketed through simple supply and demand. Local and regional advertisers started disappearing because they couldn't afford the higher rate and the market became dominated by larger national companies. Since these large advertisers were already large and had national distribution; the results from these TV commercials were huge; so they happily paid the money. Today February 2, 2014 is the Super bowl, and the cost for advertising on this program is 4 million for 30 seconds. They still think TV is a good deal I presume.

As the advertising prices rose the length of the average commercial shrank down and down until it finally got to an average of 30 seconds; you may or not remember but they used to be about two minutes long. So here's why this is all important to you; with only 30 seconds available advertisers lost the opportunity to really educate their prospects. There was no time available; so instead they started using slogans, they did not explain why they were better, what their unique selling proposition was or what they gave them a competitive edge instead it was all slogans and clichés; simply because of lack of time.

Large advertisers discovered that because there were relatively few competitors, competing on a national stage they could just spend money and win automatically; they didn't have to be better, they didn't have to be unique, they didn't have to offer better service or quality, they could simply pony up the big bucks in TV commercials and then laugh all the way to the bank. If there were a few competitors that was fine; there was enough business to split two or three ways; this is why we ended up with two or three major players in most national industries.

We have GM and Chrysler, Pepsi and Coke et cetera; ultimately what happened is advertisers lost their sales and marketing function and instead became all about creativity and design. Hey, let's create something funny, cute, entertaining and then imprint it on everybody's brains by playing it a billion times on TV and we'll win.

Melts in your mouth and on your hand, like a good neighbour, State farm is there, don't leave home without it, fly the friendly skies, how about this one, don't squeeze the... That's right, don't squeeze the Charmin. How did you know that; that commercial hasn't run for several decades? Anyhow creativity, slogans and clichés took over and began to fill every advertising medium; radio, newspaper, magazines, billboard's, Yellow Pages; you name it. In fact they even teach this kind of junk in business colleges and universities, because they think this is the way to do it. After all, these companies have made their millions doing marketing this way it must be right, right? Yeah not quite, not even close.

So here is the big problem, nearly everybody today involved in advertising and marketing including marketing graduates, marketing directors, business owners and advertising salespeople all grew up in an era of creativity, slogans and clichés. So what do they do when it's time to create their own marketing and advertising? They call upon the memory banks and pull up all the marketing and advertising they've ever seen in their life and use it as a model to create their own advertising and marketing; the result is that they come up with a bunch of clichés and lame slogans. It's the invisible gorilla in the advertising industry; everybody is doing it the wrong way, even in your industry but here is the beautiful part about it all, the best ones fix this problem.

If you take a step back and look at the market place again you'll see that there's a big gorilla pounding his chest at you; if you just follow the methodology I've taught you; you can take your company on the path towards total dominance.

Chapter 3: The Sales funnel

Now before we get too far down the line I need to bring an important concept to light for you, I want to talk about something we call the sales funnel. Now I know you've heard that term before but don't chew me out here because the sales funnel means something different in The Total Dominance vernacular than what you may be thinking of. I want to change your definition of this term so it more appropriately lines up with the concept of marketing systems. I want to get through this quickly so I need you to go through a mental exercise with me.

I want you draw a line in your mind with a point on each end. The point on the far left has a value of 1 and the point on the far right has a value of 100, okay. So now you've got a line representing points 1 through 100 from left to right, this line represents what we call the sales funnel. Point one represents the point at which your prospect starts thinking about buying whatever it is that you sell, or possibly switching vendors if it's something that they already buy. Point 100 represents the point at which they actually make the purchase and buy whatever it is that you sell.

So what you need to realize here is that there's a process, a timeline, a sales funnel that your prospect goes through before they make a purchase. That sales funnel is represented by this line, the time it takes for someone to go from point 1 to point 100 could be one day or it could be one year or more, it all depends. But the point is that you need to recognise that this sale cycle exists.

Think about it like this, point 25 or so represents when your prospect starts checking out your product in stores or noticing ads for your product or service. Around points 50-60 is where the prospect might start looking at the differences between competitors and perhaps even doing some online comparison shopping point 80-90 or so represents that point at which the prospect has determined that he's going to buy. At that point it's not a matter of if he's going to buy; but just when and from whom.

So there are two very important things to recognise about the sales funnel. First you must recognise that your job as a marketer is to push your prospects down along the sales funnel and to control the process; all the while you make your prospects feel like they're in control. Your job is to facilitate the decision-making process or to simply ensure that your prospects are moving along the sales funnel and heading towards your front door.

The second thing you must recognize is that at any given moment in time, the number of prospects who have made the decision to buy represents the smaller number of people on the sales funnel. In other words in your entire pool of prospects, there are anywhere from 5 to 10 times more people who haven't made the decision to buy anything yet. We call this group of people future buyers; those who have made the decision to buy represented by point 80-90 or so, those are what we call now buyers.

So here is an awesome tip that I want you to think about very carefully; 90% of all advertising you see or hear targets the now buyers. Why? Because they're already in the market to buy so any advertisement about a product or service that they are planning on buying already will naturally get some results just because the ad was there. This is why most ads can get by being so terrible, because no matter how bad the advertisement is, as long as there's a market for your product or service, there will always be at any given time the number of prospects on the far right side of the sales funnel who will respond to poorly created advertising material just because it showed up. But you're only making money with this type of advertising based on the force of the market. If the market is moving you can make money just by showing up. Hey, people are going to buy a product or service and if you just show up some percentage of those people buy from you. It's just the force of the market, as long as the market is moving you can sell to it.

As little kids we had a saying for this, we used to say "sh**" flows downhill. I know it's kind of gross but hey, we were kids. But the point is this; even something that is worthless and should be discarded will move if the conditions are right. Is that really what you want? Do you really want to just subsist on the force of the market or do you want to dominate?

The Local Market Domination program is not designed for people who just want to get by and make some money and have just enough just to pay the bills; we promote to thrive not to just survive. No, the "Local Market Dominance" program was created for people who were willing to do whatever it takes as long as it's legal, moral and ethical to be number one.

We're looking for individuals who believe that Total Market Dominance is their mission... to be the very best they can be, who want to surpass the competition to the point they have no hope of ever catching up. Who are ready and willing to handle the success that comes from their diligence and determination, and who looks forward to blessing others with the rewards of their own success? Look, running a business isn't for pussies. It's serious, it's hard work and it takes a commitment. I'll talk more about this towards the end of the book, but for now let's talk about this in regards to the sales funnel (funnel).

You see if you only target those now buyers at the end of the sales funnel (funnel), your advertising and marketing campaigns will be like a drug. You'll run some ads, get some results and then as soon as the ads stop your new sales will stop.

In 2006 I developed a licensee program called "Back in Action". My mistake was allowing it to be a democracy. We had at one time 58 Chiropractors following the program, and as would happen when the strength in numbers became apparent, the group got together and decided to save money by scaling down their advertising (thinking they owned the market), they decided collectively to save money and make the promotions smaller thinking their numbers would be the dominating factor, rather than maintaining the per person investment and scaling up to total market dominance.

As the result, attracting new clients to their clinics began to drop, and rather than noticing the scale down affect was causing the lack of response, they were insistent on the ads being no longer effective. As the down spiral continued one by one they dropped out, saying the marketing didn't work anymore until the group disbanded. At the same time another individual saw the opportunity and scaled up! That group now dominates that market that the first group originally dominated!

Thinking it marketing and advertising has to always be new to be able to get more business is just like a drug. You have to constantly start new campaigns so you can get your fix.

Now look, I'm not necessarily opposed to constantly running advertising campaign especially if that makes financial sense, but the point here is that this situation only occurs because you're targeting the smallest portion of people on the sales funnel. Think about what would happen if you were targeting 100% of the people on the sales funnel; everybody from 1-100 not just those at the end?

What if you had a system in place that automatically followed up with all your prospects controlling the marketing prospects and pushing your prospects down the sales funnel to your front door without any effort on your part?

Well I'm going to show you exactly how to do this. Read the book in its entirety and by the time you're finished you'll know how to target 100%

of your prospects, including both future buyers and now buyers and you'll be on your way towards total market dominance.

Chapter 4: Innovation

Okay so now we've identified some of the problems with existing advertising and marketing let's talk about the solution. The solution to these marketing and advertising problems is the Local Market Domination program. This program is entirely original. it combines some of the best elements of multiple, well-known marketing systems and experts to create one complete and cohesive marketing system, that gives your business the leverage to dominate your market place. So it is quite possible that a few elements of what I'm going to discuss here and there may sound similar to things that you've heard, but I'm confident that you have not heard anything like what I'm about to share with you. We've put it all together and developed a comprehensive system that gives you the leverage you need to rise to total dominance.

So there are five major components of the Local Market Dominance program I am going to reveal them one by one.

Component one is business innovation:

Believe it or not your very first marketing opportunity comes down to what you offer the market as a business. In other words what is it about your company that is unique and distinctive, which give your customers a reason to buy from you instead of anyone of your competitors?

People call this a unique selling point or a USP, the idea here is that you need something that is legitimately unique about your business that makes people feel that they should buy from you; Something that lets people know that you not just a commodity... you're not just like everybody else.

I call this a business innovation because the best way to come up with a USP; unique selling point is to innovate your business, service or product and to give the marketplace exactly what they want. Plus once you come up with something you truly innovative it's incredibly simple to write headlines about innovation.

Let me give you a few examples, let's say you innovative a car and you created a car that runs on water instead of gas or electricity, pretty innovative right? What would you say in the ads, what would be your headline? I've got it, how about its efficient and environmentally friendly status? No of course not, you see how utterly ridiculous those clichés sound? That's basically the equivalent of what most companies today are doing.

Building great businesses with incredible products and services, then telling the market place that they are efficient and environmentally friendly, in other words, use clichés? No! Writing a headline for innovative products and services is easy; you simply make being the innovation a big fat headline. For example in the case of a car that runs on water, use a headline that says..."This car runs on water"!

I might add the sub headline that says, seriously! So the headline and sub headline would be huge and it would say, this car runs on water! Seriously! Of course there will be a picture of the car there. See how that passes the three cliché evaluations, it's not something you expect so it passes the, I would hope so test. Certainly no one else can say it and it definitely passes the cross out write-in test you're talking about a car that runs on water for crying out loud it's more than innovative, it's enough to change the world.

Now that's an over exaggerated example; using extremely innovative product concepts but it's easy to come up with an innovation; you simply have to ask yourself one simple question, what does my marketplace want or need that nobody is offering them? It's that simple but here's the catch; you must answer the question without regards to your ability to build on those needs just ask a question and answer it. Don't tell yourself, well I can't do that because it's too expensive, I don't have the manpower or the experience, whatever, just answer the question. Once you have the answer figure out how to give it your customers. You might not be able to give them 100% of what they want, but even if you give them 50% it's better than anybody else and it makes you innovative.

Let's look at another example of innovation, competition on a local level with contractors is pretty fierce, one of my friends is a heating and air conditioning contractor. We determined that one of the biggest problems with his industry is that people feel uncomfortable with most service technicians that come to the home to repair their furnace or air conditioning system, so what's the answer to this problem?

Well most contractors say that the technicians are all background checked and drug tested and they wouldn't send anybody to your house that they wouldn't want themselves.

Take a look in your area and you'll find these kinds of clients, but here's the problem, it's the rule cliché. I mean who else can say that? How about everybody, they all say that the technicians are background checked and drug tested, and guess what?

Did you know that over 80% of heating and air condition technicians learned their trade in prison because it's the second most commonly taught trade in prison? That means that when a repair technician is in your house with your wife and kids it's an over 80% likelihood that he is an ex con; how comfortable does that make you feel?

So we innovated the business and produced a code of ethics and competency guide for heating and air conditioning companies, it is a one-page document, lists 20 requirements that the technicians must have, which includes the obvious things like back checks and drug tests and additional items, minimum standards, personal requirements, dress code and appearance; it even guarantees that the customer will receive $100 cash on the spot if a technician uses profanity while on the job.

Now we can simply advertise that our company is the only company in the state that requires all of the service technicians to be certified in the code of ethics and competency; and it is the guide to using air conditioner companies; who else can say that? Nobody! Does it pass the, well I would hope so test? Yes. Does it pass the cross out write in test? Yes. We did the same thing with one of another of my clients who's a plumber.

There are the same problems and fears in the plumbing industry; in fact the stigma to plumbers is even worse and remember over 90% of plumbers out there today earn their trade in prison. In this case my client wasn't willing to be as aggressive as the heating and Air Conditioning Company but ended up creating something similar.

In this case it's called the customer's bill of rights for the plumbing industry; again it was recommended they create a one-page document listing a whole bunch of guarantees and rights that customers received when doing business with the plumber with the pitch; Our plumbers are proud to abide by the customer's Bill of Rights for the plumbing industry which protects you the customer from having any negative experiences that they might otherwise have with an ordinary plumbing company. Who else can say that? Nobody, does it, they hit on a hot button for the marketplace about getting ripped off by a plumber?

Are there other companies in your marketplace that's doing anything like it? Yes, there is in some markets, definitely not all, it is rather innovative in marketing. Though, I have seen these tactics in marketing with carpet cleaners, moving companies, plumbers, air conditioning companies and more and more companies that require an intimate encounter in your home.

Does it increase the marketplace awareness that it is possible to have a very negative experience with an in home service company while simultaneously increasing the confidence that those following a code of ethics has effectively solved this problem and will protect you from a possibly negative experience? Yes and that's the key, it increases the confidence that people really want.

Imagine the trust we put into companies that install security in your home, wouldn't you want to be assured they are very reputable, after all they have all the passcodes and know when you are not home.

People want the unshakeable confidence that your company, product or service is the very best in terms of value and safety; and they don't want to feel like they got ripped off, like they could have got a better deal.

This brings us to this incredibly important point, so remember what I'm about to say right now. *The amount of money that somebody is willing to give you is directly proportionate to their confidence in your ability to provide them with the goods and services they want and need,* period. I will discuss the "tripwire" effect later in the book to emphasize this point.

Let me say that for the sake of emphasis; the amount of money some is willing to give you is directly proportionate to their confidence in your ability to provide them with the goods and services that they want or need.

Now I am sure you have heard that the way to increase profits is to increase the value or perceived value that you offer your customers, I'm here to tell you this type of thinking is antiquated and outmoded, flat-out wrong.

By wrong, I mean that it's missing a critical element, the missing element is confidence; this is actually what people buy. Not to de-value the value of results, but the more confidence I have in your ability to provide me with the goods and services I want or need, the more value you have in my eyes and the more money I will be willing to give you.

Too many people think that the way to increase prices and value is to add additional products and services, but this is the wrong methodology. Invest your time, energy and resources into increasing people's confidence in your product and services and your price points and profits will increase. |

The key is confidence, for example would you buy a big Mac at McDonald's for 20 bucks no, why not? Because you know it's not worth 20 bucks, what if McDonald's added value to the big Mac by adding a large fries and a Coke for free now would you buy the big mac for $20? Of course not, what if they added more value by giving a free happy meal still the answer is no, why?

Because you know that no matter what additional free stuff they add it's still not worth the 20 bucks you would spend to buy a fillet minion steak from a major steakhouse. The 20 bucks of course would be a deal at the steakhouse, just not at McDonalds, but why the difference? The big Mac is said to be made out of 100% pure beef and so is the fillet so why are you willing to buy one and not the other? Because you're by reputation you are confident that one of them is worth more than $20 and the other is not, it's that simple.

Winning the game of business and sales is an issue of confidence, perception of value and both consequences of confidence; so invest in building your market's confidence in your company, your products and your services and you'll be on your way to total market dominance.

Obviously in terms of innovation there's a big difference between a car that runs on water and the code of ethics and competency guide for heating and air companies or the customer's bill of rights for the plumbing industry and that's the point. I want you to see and realize that while they're very different in terms of value, they're exactly the same in terms of principle.

The principle here is to write something innovative to the marketplace they actually want and need. Now it's possible that you already have something innovative in your business if that's the case then it's incredibly important to present this innovation as something unique to the marketplace, you should name it and trademark it and make it the brand of your company.

Here is one more example; I have heard of one of one of the oldest emergency food supplier companies in the country. They have provided nitrogen packs and sealed food for 40 years now. Normally saying you've been in business for 40 years is a major cliché it's basically meaningless but in this case it actually matters and here's why.

Most emergency food supply companies advertise their food lasts 10, 15 or 20 years but the companies themselves haven't even been in business that long to know that, do they?

This company has been in business for over 40 years, they've actually tested their food after 20, 25 and 30 years and it's still good; They know because they have had the opportunity to taste some of their 30-year-old food; that is definitely a unique selling proposition to be brought to light.

Here is a tool that you can use to create your own business innovations. We actually have innovation formulas that we use that allow us to easily and scientifically find needs and desires in any industry or marketplace and then create unique innovations to fill those needs and desires that can easily be implemented by our clients. Some are more advanced than others but in every case a true and exclusive business innovation is developed so that our clients distinguish themselves in the marketplace.

I would like to share one of these innovations with you; this one is called the ultimate solution, it's remarkably simple yet powerful. I even named a company I started "The Total weight loss Solution, and with a subheading it worked very well.

Another innovation for a chiropractic office was, Back In Action. It was a play on words of sort , yet the marketing focused on our office as the solution when you are out of the action... physically, that our office will get you back in action! I was copied maybe thousands of times (the "me too" copy trend) by others using a similar phrase, like "back in alignment", yet the phrase didn't carry the weight, or promote a wanted benefit, (the public does not see alignment as a benefit without further education on your service) there marketing didn't support the power of the message we presented, our name implied the benefit!

All you need to do is write down on a piece of paper a negative situation that your customers could always have in doing business with someone in your industry.

Think of a dentist and write down the negative experiences that people could have with a dentist, now that reputation marketing is in my wheel house; I read a lot of negative reviews, problems relating to fear or financial misunderstandings, problems with insurance payments or just having to wait too long. Whatever seems to be the hurdle one must jump to make a client happy?

Write down the potential negative experiences, then ask yourself this killer question; if your customers have the power to change anything in your business to solve this problem what would they do to alleviate the problem? In other words, what would the ultimate business do to ensure that this problem never existed?

What is the ultimate solution? Brainstorm answers to this question with everybody, just let it go, write everything down on paper; do not exclude any ideas just because they're not practical. In fact if at least 50% of your ideas are not impractical then you'll never innovate anything significant so for the sake of this book, I use a ridiculously simple example so you can understand the methodology here and in the real world I want to come up with much better innovations.

In this example let's evaluate the dentist really quick in the waiting experience. The problem here is that people have an appointment and they show up on time and then they had to wait 15 to 20 minutes before they're seen. We need some innovations. How about guarantee that if you are not seen within five minutes of your scheduled appointment time, you will receive a free tooth whitening!

Or how about a free neck massage while you wait, If a dentist had someone give me a neck massage while I was waiting for my appointment I'd actually look forward to every appointment and get there early, I'd also brag about my great dentist to everybody I know.

How about this, 50 different magazines in the waiting area in all categories with current issues, how about wireless internet connections to your laptop, computer stations with internet, how about instead of waiting room have a home theatre setup playing IMAX documentaries all day, have a leather recliner, all snacks and drinks are free or video games and video simulators! Truly not all of those would be correct for all situations, but I hope you get the picture!

If at least half your ideas aren't crazy or impractical you'll never come up with anything good so just let your mind go and see all ideas as being possible. Remember to think with the end in mind is to ensure that the business innovation you come up with builds your customer's confidence in your ability to provide them with an amazing experience while they receive your goods and services.

Here's a final point I want to make about innovation. Innovation is not just a business function, it's actually a core part of your marketing program, simply put, if you want to dominate your sector of the market you must be innovative, I like to think in terms of the practice or business culture. Have the TEAM wear the products you promote, or be good examples of living the culture you promote. In a Chiropractic setting I promote what I refer to as "Lifestyle management; since most of the trending infirmities are caused by lifestyle choices. The culture of the office is "living a healthy lifestyle" and sells services which promote health.

Choices for the clients then can be to observe your TEAM and choose the Lifestyle that will result closest to their health goals. By their utilization of the services provided by the clinic as well as possible eating or exercise choices... Consider this... if your "culture' is health, how do you feel it would impact those considering your services if the TEAM and the doctor exude health and are living examples of the products they recommend? Of course you would be living examples which will cause others to have confidence in your service and want to join your culture. This is marketing... it comes with little to no cost, and is responsible to attract the best new clients through referral!

You cannot expect to win the lion share of the market place by being just like everybody else, furthermore you can't just be different for the sake of being different your innovation must address the real and legitimate wants and/or needs of your target market.

Chapter 5: Strategic Messaging Formula

Okay, so now that we've identified some of the problems with existing advertising and marketing, let's talk about the solutions. I want to show you exactly what you're marketing content is supposed to look like. Believe it or not the process of creating effective and strategic marketing programs is actually scientific; you've been taught to believe that marketing is an art, and that you need a team of creative people to invent funny, quirky, entertaining or any other type of creative content to use in your advertising and marketing; but this is simply not the case.

Years ago there was a marketing acronym used called AIDA it stood for Attention Interest Desire and Action in Rich Harshaw's book called 'Monopolise your Marketplace; Rich uploaded this formula and called it the Marketing Equation.

Both of these systems worked well for years and still do; however in today's Internet age, with so much information being disseminated online and with the incredible software tools available to us along with our own testing in the Local Market Domination program we have refined this system even further.

We call this scientific method of creating comprehensive marketing systems, the Local market domination formula and we use it exclusively within the Local Market Domination system, to generate industry leading results for all our customers; no matter the industry.

Ultimately the goal of the local market domination formula is to cause your customers and prospects to draw this important conclusion that you've heard several times already. **"I'd have to be completely insane to work with anyone except you, no matter the price."** Don't you want your customers and prospects thinking that way? Of course you do! So let me show you how this works.

The local market domination formula or SMF for short has five components, let me introduce them to you really quick.

First is Acquire, this means that you must first acquire your target market's attention; I call a new prospective client a Suspect rather than a prospect, because the public is suspicious at best about your unique service. You may think by there simply being there it is obvious they may be interested in what you have to sell, but in fact they usually need way more understanding to make a buying decision to become a prospective client. This may seem confusing and not as easy as it should be to pull off as you may think; yet this understanding which was ultimately put into the new client on-boarding procedure was responsible for my over 90% conversion rate of new patients to my office.

Furthermore, the connection process is done wrong more often than it is done right, and may be responsible for the industry wide constant need of new patients, because of low conversion and low referral numbers. Plus the mistake of thinking price is the real reason for not accepting a Core Offer. When someone says, boy that sounds good, but I just cannot afford it, it may have a little truth to it, so the proper response is to make payment arrangements to increase affordability, but when you totally miss it, and they have no clue as to your value and benefit you provide, they just use no time or money as a politically correct excuse... They just don't believe you. You'll learn how, what and why in a few minutes. This is illustrated in more detail as the Lead Magnet in the last chapter.

The second component is Connection; this means that once you've captured your prospects attention you must connect with them on an emotional level. You have to hold on to their attention by connecting the hot button that is important or relevant to them. You have to make them feel important or relevant while delivering the decision making information they need; information that will help them make the best decision possible. In short you will be helping to facilitate the decision-making process through your communication efforts.

The third component is Inform, now that you've connected with your prospects on an emotional level you must give them enough quality information to make them feel like they can make an informed decision about how to solve their problem, or gain a needed benefit, through the utilization of your service.

You do this by giving your prospect enough quality information to address their emotional needs. Remember the component is called *inform*, so you are informing them; this step is ultra-critical and it turns the sale from an emotional sale to a logical one.

The fourth component is *Incentivize*; in this step you have to give your prospect an incentive to get to the next step in the buying process. That is often accomplished by giving your prospect an offer to get a free marketing tool of some sort; like a special report, a book, series of videos, audio program or anything like that. I will explain deeper when I talk about the trip wire effect in the last chapter.

However you should never give away a marketing tool; often you can give them a coupon, exclusive discounts, special limited opportunities or any other low risk or high value offer, but your goal is to have them make a low risk purchase as soon as possible, which now transforms them form looker/prospect to buyer/client.

Whatever it is just remember that you are incentivizing your prospect, you want them to take the next step in the buying process.

The Fifth and final component is **Automate**, this simply means that now your prospects are connected with you and you're marketing system, you must create content to automate the follow-up process.

This will be covered once again in the last chapter as I teach you, the return path. Companies and individuals are notoriously bad about following up. Fortunately software is available today to assist in this process, but even then the software will not give you the best bang for your buck if you don't properly craft your message and follow-up sequence. We're going to show you exactly how to accomplish this in the next few chapters.

The acronym for the local market domination formula is CCIIA; the easiest way to remember it is to think of the CIA but with two C's and two I's. Just like the CIA is the Central intelligence agency of the United States, the world's greatest superpower; so the local market domination formula is the brains and centre of your comprehensive marketing system. Capture, Connect, Inform, Incentivise and Automate. My short and easier to remember formula is ACT. Acquire, connect and Transform. It's a proven formula for marketing success. It's a scientific approach to marketing that is based on human nature, and when properly executed drives your prospects and customers to this conclusion.

Go ahead and say the next sentence out loud to remember your marketing purpose... The response in the mind of our prospect should be saying... "**I have to be completely insane to work with anybody else but you, no matter the price.**" So let's break down each of the components of the strategic messaging formula.

Chapter 6: Modern Neuroscience

Okay now before I break down the five components of the local market domination formula I need to give you a quick lesson in modern studies of neurological science; don't worry this is not that technical, even though I might use some big scientific words. Yes this is incredibly important when it comes to marketing and understanding what I'm about to share with you. It will be the big difference between whether or not you just get by like everyone else in the marketplace or if you completely dominate your market place. So pay attention, this is important stuff.

The first big scientific term that I need to introduce you to is the reticular activating system or RAS for short. Now the reticular activating system is basically a part of your brain that controls certain functions of consciousness; more specifically the RAS is a loose network of neurons and neural fibers running through the brain stem; these neurons connect with other various parts of the brain.

Functions of the reticular activating system are many and varied; studies actually show that it contributes to the control of sleep, walking, sex, eating and even elimination, but the most important function of the RAS is its control of your consciousness. You see it is believed that the RAS, reticular activating system controls your functions of sleep, wakefulness and your ability to consciously focus attention on something. Additionally the RAS acts as a filter, dampening down the effects of impeding stimuli like loud noises; which allows you to focus and also helps to prevent your senses from being overloaded.

So what in the world does that have to do with marketing, well everything. Think about what I just described about your own brain; there's actually a part of your brain that filters out what you pay attention to and what to disregard, and it's called the reticular activating system.

It should be obvious that your goal in marketing is to make your prospects reticular activating system your best friend. You want their RAS to pay attention to you, your company and your products and services and to disregard everything else. It's a pretty simple goal but making that happen isn't necessarily as easy, but I'm going to teach you exactly how to do that when we walk through the strategic messaging formula; then you'll understand much better about how and why the Local Market Domination program is a scientific approach to marketing as opposed to simply a creative approach. So before I can explain how to get into the heads or your prospects RAS; from now on I will just call the reticular activating system the RAS; to be your best friend; I need to explain specifically.

We need to talk about alpha brain waves and beta brainwaves; seriously scientists have discovered that your brain is made up of billions of brain cells called neurons and these neurons actually communicate with one another using electricity. This electrical communication can actually be detected and measured using a piece of medical equipment called an electroencephalogram or EEG; which was invented by Doctor Hans Berger. Researchers noted that this electrical brain activity operates in a rhythm; these brainwaves actually correspond with certain known functions of everyday life.

There are two types of brain waves that are relevant to us; they are alpha brainwaves and beta brainwaves. Now alpha brainwaves are measured when we're calm, relaxed and in a normal state of awareness; in other words you're not really paying close attention to any one thing. This is your brain's automatic mode of performing everyday regular tasks without any real conscious effort.

For this reason I call alpha brainwaves auto mode since these brainwaves allow you to function on autopilot. For example; have you ever driven to work and not paid any attention to where you were going but miraculously you've got to work, how? It happened because your brain automatically took you there without any conscious effort.

On a conscious level you might have been listening to the radio, shaving, grabbing down a burger or whatever it is that you do; maybe even talking on your cell phone using a speakerphone or other hands-free device, just doing whatever you do. But your brain is automatically driving you to work; so thank God for this autopilot mode of consciousness because it allows us to function very well.

However think about what this means in terms of marketing. You see your prospects might see or hear your ads with their eyes and ears but not actually pay attention to it. Think about all forms of media whether it's print, TV, Internet or whatever; the vast majority of ads get lost because they're only seen on the alpha level, meaning your brain didn't really pay attention to it.

Remember the invisible gorilla we talked about earlier; yeah Alpha brainwaves shut it out of your view because you were paying attention to something else. Alpha brainwave is what I call auto mode it's pretty easy to understand; let's move on to beta brainwaves or what I call conscious mode. Now beta brainwaves kick in when you're thinking logically, feeling stressed or feeling tense; it's your brain states active mental engagement in intentional consciousness.

You've got beta brainwaves moving when you're trying to solve a difficult math problem, when you're driving in a thunderstorm or slippery roads, when you're inching towards the edge of your seat as the movie you're watching starts coming to a climax or when you're plotting your own market domination!

But seriously you need to understand the beta brainwaves or what I call conscious mode is when your brain is paying attention. So the point in all this and I hope this is obvious now, is to snap your prospects out of auto mode and into conscious mode; and we need to get the brainwaves out of alpha rhythm and into beta rhythm and fortunately for you there are scientific ways to make this happen.

It's not as complicated as you think; in fact, street magicians and pickpockets have used this to their advantage over the years they've learned how to get people to focus on one thing while they pick your pockets, steal your watch or amaze you with some trick; but understand that they can only do these tricks because they're taking advantage of your brains levels of consciousness.

Now I want to show you a scientific method; using this to your advantage as you develop a marketing system, in short all you have to do to get your prospect out of alpha auto mode and into data conscious mode is to get the attention of the RAS. Remember, that's the reticular activating system; the RAS is constantly on the lookout on a subconscious level 24 hours a day; even while you're sleeping. The things that fall into one of these three categories are things that are familiar, things that are unusual and things that are problematic got it? So whenever the RAS detects any of these things on a subconscious level it sends a message to the conscious side of your brain that basically says; Hey, pay attention or check this out. Now whatever those things are, those things that are familiar, unusual or problematic, we call them activators.

Let me give you some examples of activators in real life. When was the last time you bought a new car, not necessarily a car that was new but one that was new to you; once you bought the car how often did you see that same kind of car on the road? A lot right? You may have never even noticed it before, what about meeting new friends; let say his name is Fred, who drives say a green Toyota Camry. We may have never noticed that the Green Camry ever existed, but now you see them all over town and every time you see one it forces you to pay close attention; you look to see if it is Fred driving that car, well that's the reticular activating system at work because your new car or your friends car is familiar to you and the car has become an activator.

When your subconscious radar picks one out of the crowd it pokes the conscious side of the brain and says hey, check that out, before, when the Green Camry wasn't familiar the brain would just see another sedan on a subconscious level and it wouldn't notify you of anything. Back before you met Fred with the Green Camry, the Camry wasn't an activator; Because it wasn't familiar, unusual or problematic. So you've probably already figured out that to get your prospects attention you just need some activators that are familiar, unusual or problematic in your ads and then what? Well slow down, cool your jets supercharge; it's not that easy.

Let me explain to you the biggest mistake people make in this process; because they try to mimic the jokers who run Madison Avenue. These schmucks usually prefer to use activators that are based on things that are familiar and unusual because they're the easiest things to pull off.

For example, have you ever noticed how many animals there are in advertising; Energizer has a bunny, AFLAC has a duck, Merrill Lynch has a Bull, Microsoft used to use a butterfly, Budweiser used to use frogs and Horses. The point is most creative agencies use animals because they are likeable and familiar and they cause your RAS to pay attention.

Now the same goes for celebrities; celebrities are familiar right; I mean by definition a celebrity is famous, meaning they are familiar to lots of people. Now it is true that celebrities add credibility to your company and your product, but more importantly they capture your attention because the RAS detects something familiar and says pay attention! Once you're paying attention the company now is in a position to sell you something.

That's the typical junk that you see coming out of creative agencies, their goal and purpose is to come up with something so strange, so odd, so shocking, so flat-out unusual that it captures your RAS's attention; the bad news is that we become more and more desensitised to strange things; So those creative jokers have to create things that are increasingly more strange.

What about sexuality and marketing; you've heard that sex sells right, well that's not totally true. You see sexy things actually capture your attention because it's detected by your RAS but it doesn't necessarily sell; quite plainly using sex is a shameless and distasteful way to capture prospects attention and it is one that we will never use in the Local Market Domination System.

So what have we learned here, we've learned about your reticular activating system or RAS, we've learned about your brains brainwaves and more specifically how we must capture the attention of you RAS and cause you to snap out of alpha auto mode into beta conscious mode. We also learned that you do this by using activators, which are things that are familiar, unusual or problematic. Now I want to teach you how to find and create the right activators and put this knowledge to work for you in your business.

Chapter 7: Capture

Now let's talk about the first component of the strategic messaging formula; as a reminder it is capture. This is the most obvious component of the formula but I can tell you that it's done wrong more often than not; in fact this is really one of the major areas of false doctrine that you're going to have to unlearn if you really want to rise to a place of total dominance.

You see large corporations and their Madison Avenue ad agencies have been using all types of strange creative methods for years to get your attention and unfortunately the memory of these advertising methods is stuck in your head so you're likely to follow this lead since you really don't know any different.

Today is the super bowl and this type of advertising will speak loudly at 4 million for 30 seconds. Budweiser has the frogs and the lizards. In the past Pepsi used Britney Spears practically naked and they used the late and great Michael Jackson with his hair on fire, Geico has a talking gecko and years ago Mr Whipple used to tell us not to squeeze the Charmin, and we cannot forget the old lady who used to ask us, where's the beef?

Anyhow this kind of advertising is often called pattern interrupt advertising because it's designed to interrupt our robotic nature and cause us to pay attention. They're using the RAS to their advantage by utilising things that are familiar or unusual.

But here's the thing, even though these ad agencies are effectively using activators to snap people out of auto mode into conscious mode, most people quit paying attention because the content of their ad is not important or relevant to them. I mean really do you care about a talking gecko? No, you don't; it might be entertaining but it's not important.

So the only way these advertising agencies can get people to really pay attention or remember the ads is to play the ad as many times as possible and the ad agencies love this because they make a commission every time their clients buy an ad.

So the ad agencies tell their clients, "Mr./Mrs. Client, we have this ridiculously entertaining ad with a rat terrier wrestling a giant Rat and it's been focus tested to get people's attention and everybody thinks it's really funny.

In order to really make this campaign work we'll need to spend about $500,000 a week on advertising over the next few months." You see, the only way these ridiculous ads stick in your mind is by pure repetition, they have to play the ads again and again and again. A practice the average entrepreneur just can't afford.

This reminds me of the story of the advertising executive who was trying to promote some products in South America. He got a call from one of his associates who proudly proclaimed that they got 2 Brazilian TV stations to run their ads, the executive responded boy that's fantastic, so now tell me, how many Brazilian's will watch? Is it close to a million! Think about it, if you throw enough mud at the wall some of it is going to stick and that is what people are doing with the ads that you're familiar with. They're just throwing as much mud at the wall as possible and they're profiting from it greatly; they make more and more money by spending your money.

When you don't get good results they simply respond by reassuring you that the ads created awareness. That's right, awareness, you've heard this before.

Awareness is fine and dandy but I'm more interested in sales and revenue, what would you rather have? Increased awareness or more business?

Think about it, when you focus your efforts on actually generating revenue you will simultaneously create awareness as well. I personally am quite disgusted with most ad agencies and I'm constantly exposing their tactics. Yes it's true, but I would rather empower the market place and let people make their own decisions as to what they want to do and what model they should use.

The standard commission in the industry is 15% on medium buys; in other words an ad agency is going to make a 15% commission on the ads that you buy so how can you really trust an ad agency to give you solid advice about how many ads you should run? The answer is simple, you can't. I mean, everything looks like a nail when you are holding a hammer right? To an ad agency all of your marketing problems are solved by just spending more money on ads.

The ad agency model is 100 years old and it is simply outdated, antiquated and as far as I'm concerned flat out wrong. We don't think you should do business with somebody who makes their money by spending yours. The Local Market Domination model is different, our compensation is tied to your businesses growth, and it's really simple. If we don't grow your business you don't pay. How can we do this? Simple, our methods work and by the time you're done with this book you'll understand how and why.

Chapter 8: Hot Buttons

So let's get into the meat and potatoes; in short we need to use hot buttons. Many people have different definitions of what a hot button is our definition is simple; hot button is an activator that is important or relevant to the prospect. Now remember an activator is something that is familiar unusual or problematic and it snaps people out of auto mode into conscious mode; those activators cause your RAF to send you a signal that says hey, pay attention.

The most important thing here is to get your prospect to not only pay attention but to remain interested; this is the big key that's missing in nearly all the ads that you've seen, that have otherwise successfully captured people's attention.

If you get this part of the process right you'll be light years ahead of the competition. Let me give you some examples; let's say you did see one of Cokes billboards with the polar bear drinking Coke, it might capture your attention because the animal's familiar and is doing something unusual but when the brain seeks for any clarifying information that makes it important or relevant it finds nothing, so you were back quickly into auto mode; you see how that works.

Let me define a hot button for you one more time for sake of clarity hot button is an activator that is also important or relevant to the prospect. Remember anything that catches the reticular activating system's attention and pulls someone out of alpha auto mode and into beta conscious mode because it's familiar, unusual or problematic is considered an activator button. An activator is only a hot button if it's also important or relevant, this is critical.

If you're not using hot buttons in your advertising then you're not maximising your results of your marketing and here's why; once your attention has been captured your brain will automatically seek additional information to determine if the thing that captured your attention is important or relevant to you; if it is, then you continue to pay attention. If not then you're back to Alpha auto mode and you will likely not buy the product or service that was being advertised.

Earlier I mentioned that the large Madison Avenue agencies like to use activators that are familiar or unusual and that's fine with me because it means that their results will always be under leveraged.

My advice to you is to use the hot buttons not just activators that are problematic to your target market; let me give you an example. There is a man named Matt who owns a mortgage brokerage, it was one of the top brokerage companies during the height of the real estate boom. As you may remember the boom, went boom and that company went from having a booming office, to only having only three people. In fact the local market altogether went from having 26 mortgage brokers down to four.

Matt hadn't made any money in three years and by the time he came to see what he could do had become pretty desperate to come up with something to get the business to start making sales. His idea was to create a brochure.

After going through a flash consulting session and performing a marketing leveraging analysis, it was determined that his best cause of action would be to create a complete marketing system to generate leads through direct mail. Later in this book I'll reveal what I mean by complete marketing system, but in this case the leads would first be generated by direct mail, then incentivise prospects to visit a website where they can view an offer; they will also watch a video. The sales program highlights the uniqueness of the service and offers the visitor a chance to see if they qualify for the mortgage program.

Matt was opposed to the idea of direct mail, in his view direct mail didn't work; it was too expensive and every other mortgage company was using it; but what was everybody else doing? They were sending out those letters that are gimmicks, you know, that line designed to look like they're official notes from banks or lending institutions so they can trick you into calling them and getting refinancing on your home; the market is saturated with that junk and people just aren't responding to it anymore.

So Matt was convinced to try direct mail following the same steps as we use in the Local Market Domination program, and he reluctantly agreed. The first thing was to determine what the hot buttons in his target market were; it was actually pretty simple in his case. The top three hot buttons were; people stressing out about their house payments because their payments are too high; losing their house, and they wanted to save money on their monthly mortgage payments, easy enough right.

But here's something really important to remember, different people have different hot buttons for some they just wanted to save money because they were frugal looking for ways to increase cash flow and are not necessarily stressing out about the payment.

So a mailing piece was created that addressed everybody's hot buttons. Additionally a series of postcards were created with three different headlines that addressed these three hot buttons.

Matt was really sceptical because in his view postcards don't work. To combat that objection he was shown the three reasons **why** postcards don't work for most people; one, the postcards don't use strategically formulated hot buttons that are based on relevant needs of the target market; Two the postcards are not designed as part of an overall marketing system and they only give people the option of calling instead of simply incentivising them to take the next step in the buying process, and three; most people use the wrong size and side of the postcard and are therefore ineffective.

So here's a quick marketing tip for you, use 6 x 11 postcards because it's the largest size that can fit into a standard mailbox without being folded and make sure that your headline is on the side of the postcard that has the prospects name and address; by US Postal regulations this is the side that must face the recipient; so make sure the headline is on that side.

Let me give you the three headlines that we used that each tapped into three major hot buttons. The first headline said; stop stressing out about your monthly mortgage payments. This headline was a hot button for people that were stressing about the monthly mortgage payment.

The second headline said; **save your house**, in giant letters across the top. Obviously this headline has major emotional hot button the people who are worried about losing their homes.

The third headline said, **save hundreds of dollars each month in just three easy steps**. This headline tapped into a hot button for people who simply wanted to save money each month. Remember the key here is that we're using problematic based hot buttons and not activators that are unusual or familiar. If we took that approach we could have a talking dog who says it's time to re-finance your house and my doghouse too, or you could get a celebrity to say; I just refinanced my mortgage with First Mortgage and you should too was something like that; typical creative-based marketing junk with clichés. The method was scientific, and even though it looked and sounded amazingly simple it was based on human nature and the actual relevant emotional needs of the target market.

Now obviously there's more to the system, and there is more to the postcards, that's just the gist of the program.

The first postcards were sent out on Monday and by Wednesday they had closed over $1 million in business; here are his actual words that he sent in an email, I'll read his words verbatim. "Dude, have been on the phone all day fielding these leads. I've never had anything like this, everyone is a good one and I'm not exaggerating." Later he sent a follow-up email, "over 1 million in new qualified sold loans today, that's a very, very good day." This trend continued for months as he continued the campaign; ultimately Matt got a chance to make some money, take the first vacation he had taken in many years and he had to hire five new people to handle the workload.

The point I wanted to make is that you must use hot buttons to capture people's attention, in other words activators that are either important or relevant to your target market; if you don't use hot buttons your prospects will quickly revert back to Alpha auto mode. This process of quickly reverting back into Alpha auto mode is what which Rich Harshaw called a false state, and is the most prevalent form of advertising seen today. You see how it can negatively impact your advertising dollars.

Let me give you one more example of this to make sure you understand what I'm talking about; I want to give you an example of false data that nearly everybody can relate too.

You are in a large crowd at the baggage claim at the airport. There was a lot of background noise and plenty of people. You are not necessarily planning on seeing somebody special then all of a sudden you hear an unfamiliar voice call out your name.

Say your name is Bob and you hear: "Hey Bob." What's your response? To turn around and look and of course you couldn't respond, even if you tried. The reason should be obvious after reading the last several minutes, your name is an activator it's just about the most important thing to you and as soon as you hear your name, Bob, it instantly pulls you out of auto mode and pushes you into conscious mode; and your brain immediately seeks additional information to determine if it's important or relevant to you.

You begin to wonder who it is, you try to identify the voice, what they want, how urgent does the voice sound? So what happens when you turn around and you discover that they're actually calling out to someone else who apparently has the same name as you?

This is happening to you. You then turn around and see that the person is talking to somebody else; Do you walk over there and engage that person in a conversation? No of course not, it's ridiculous and it's absurd; this is what is called false data. This example works even if you don't have a common name like Bob. My name is Bruce and it's not that common of name. So to hear that name somewhere is both unusual and familiar so it's a reticular activator double whammy.

I hope these examples illustrate for you the major problem in modern advertising and that is this; just because you've captured somebody's attention it doesn't mean you're in a position to sell them something.

Unless you can keep their attention through using hot buttons then you have zero chance of emotionally connecting with prospects, which is the next step in Local market domination formula and this is exactly what happens with most marketing today.

Even if it catches their attention it doesn't always connect with an emotional hot button, so the prospect is lost. This is one of the reasons why major advertisers have to keep changing their ad campaigns all the time; some of them even have to change the main tool they used to capture your attention like getting new celebrities.

Geico is a perfect example they've got the gecko, and they have fired the caveman it seems. Each one of those representative costs literally hundreds of millions of dollars. They also have a slogan that not everybody even hears.

When someone says fifteen minutes will save you 15% on car insurance... the other person responds, "Everybody knows that". This is their message on top of the little mascots. The ad agencies love it because they make 15% on those hundreds of millions of dollars, but in the real world the gecko enters into your brain and your brain says; it's that lame insurance ad again, don't even waste my time, and nothing happens.

When you use hot button based activators, that won't happen; a great campaign will not wear itself out" and a great campaign has to be based on a Strategic Messaging Formula; it has to have the right hot buttons and it must be a part of a complete marketing system.

Chapter 9: Connect

Component two in the Local market domination formula is connect; we basically already introduced you to this concept in the previous chapter about hot buttons, but let's dive into it a little bit deeper. The concept of connecting is pretty simple but it is incredibly important. The concept again is that after a prospect has had their attention captured, the brain will seek additional information to determine if it's important or relevant to them; if that additional clarifying information is not present the prospect will revert back to auto mode.

If there is additional information that connects with emotional hot buttons, which are relevant or important to the prospect, then the prospect will literally make a temporary emotional connection with your marketing material.

They will be completely snapped out of auto mode and they will be fully attentive to your marketing content; in short they're now paying close attention and they're in conscious mode; and you are in a position to sell them something.

Now the way to pull off the capture and connect sequence in the real world is through the use of headlines. Historically speaking you only had a second or more to really capture somebody's attention. Today in our always on world with the internet, Face Booking, text messaging, Twittering, background TV noise, news media, etc. world of flashing lights and non-stop action you've really got about a fraction of a split second to get people's attention.

It is hard to get your individual message out in this information overload world so the bottom line is that you'd better use activators that have legitimate, problematic based hot buttons; in other words use words and phrases that describe familiar problems that your prospect will likely be feeling so that the RAS will detect them and put them into conscious mode.

Now again in the real world this is accomplished through the use of headlines, everybody pretty much knows what a headline is. In print advertising like magazines, newspapers and even the dying Yellow Pages, the headline is obvious. In radio and television it's the first sentence that is spoken; in a brochure or similar piece of marketing collateral it would be the first thing they see; on a pay per click ad it's the headline on top; you get the picture.

So let me give you an example in print; I'm looking at two 8.5 x 11 brochures right now for travel companies; one of them is a typical designer based brochure with the name of the company on top it says; "The Cruise Planner". On the cover is a map of the world with pictures and it says "what in the world would you like to do", get it; what in the world and we are looking at images from the world, get it, oh it's so creative.

This is the same cliché nonsense that you will see everywhere you go; it becomes downright nauseating for me and not just because I'm a professional marketer and I eat and breathe this stuff, it is nauseating!

As a consumer it is so difficult to find the best vendor in any market since everybody says the same thing; since everybody uses clichés and nobody uses hot buttons; there are no innovative and quantifiable reasons to do business with one or the other, when they all promote the same thing!

In today's crowded business space with so many players and so much information available online the typical prospect is overwhelmed; they really want someone to cut through the clutter, capture their attention, connect with them, demonstrate that they offer a superior product or service and give them a low risk incentive to take the next step in the buying process. If you follow that method you won't just earn new business, you'll be doing your market a favour because people don't want to do the research on their own; they just want the unshakeable confidence that they chose the right company to work with in the first place.

Back to the travel agents; remember the great cliché, "what in the world would you like to do?" it's just painful. Right next to it is another travel brochure that was properly developed; this one has a giant headline that says "The five secrets of experienced travellers." Now let me walk you through a quick system for writing headlines like this, we actually have several different methods for developing powerfully articulated hot button loaded headlines. Let me just share one of the easiest ones with you and then we'll compare these headlines from these two travel agencies.

So here's what I want you to do, put yourself in the prospects shoes. I will call your prospect Pete. Now remember, Pete is the proverbial prospect, he's the guy who is going to buy whatever it is that you sell some day; maybe he's at point 10 or 15 on the sales funnel or maybe he's all the way down at point 80 or 90 and he's ready to buy right now.

No matter where Pete is at on the sales funnel, just remember that Pete is your prospect; he is going to buy what you sell some day. So now here's what you need to do; put yourself in Pete's shoes for a moment. Imagine that you are Pete and you're thinking about what is important and relevant in regards to the product or service that you want to buy.

Imagine the frustration that Pete might have about the industry or a desire that Pete might have in relation to the industry. Now what would be a statement that would come out of Pete's mouth if he were to speak out loud; whatever you think that is, write it down?

Here is another scenario. Lasik eye surgery; everybody's heard about Lasik by now; what are the major hot buttons around it? Well the top two, are price and fear, that's pretty much it. For this example let's use the fear hot button, so imagine Pete is thinking about getting Lasik, let's say he's around point 50 on the sales funnel and he's thinking about possibly getting Lasik eye surgery but he's terrified about damaging his eyes.

If he is afraid of damaging his eyes he might say something like, "I'm thinking about getting Lasik eye surgery but I'm terrified about damaging my eyes". See that? I just repeated out loud what we imagined Pete may be thinking about.

Now that statement is actually a great headline, I'll say it again; "I'm thinking about getting Lasik eye surgery but I'm terrified about damaging my eyes," that's actually a great headline. Let me show you how to rewrite that headline three times really fast so that you have a total of four headlines to work with.

Notice the statement as I said it was written in first person, now all you have to do is convert it into a question in first person instead of a statement. So the first person question would go like this, "how can I get Lasik eye surgery without damaging my eyes?" Okay got that, now let's rewrite the headline again but this time in second person; remember first person is when you are speaking and second person is when you are speaking for somebody, so you often use the word, "you" in a second person statement. In this case we are going to write the headline two times in second person; one as a statement and one as a question.

"You're thinking about getting Lasik eye surgery but you're terrified about damaging your eyes." Now as a question; "Are you thinking about getting Lasik eye surgery but you're terrified about damaging your eyes?"

See how that works; all of those are great headlines you can look them over and pick the one you think resonates best, but the point is that we just walked you through an exercise that allows you to write four powerful headlines quick.

In the real world you'll need to write multiple headlines for the different needs of your target market and you'll need to create multiple headlines for each of the three hot button categories. I haven't mentioned that there are three hot button categories that we'll review in a minute; ultimately in any marketing system you should end up with over 100 headlines from which to develop your most powerfully articulated marketing pieces.

If that sounds like a lot well it is, but I thought you were reading this book because you wanted to dominate; I thought you were willing to do what it takes to be number one. In the case of writing headlines you can't just wing it and hope for the best, you've got to do it right.

Now let me explain why this is so powerful. It is powerful because headlines and sub headlines allow you to emotionally connect with real needs and or desires that your prospect is feeling; therefore they're familiar with these needs because they have them and more often than not they're problematic as well.

Think about it, if you are thinking about getting Lasik eye surgery but you were terrified about damaging your eyes what do you think you would do if you saw an ad with a giant headline that read; "Are you think about getting Lasik eye surgery but you're terrified about damaging your eyes." You'd pay attention and stay attentive; you'd read through the entire marketing piece wouldn't you? Of course you would because it was based on human nature and your own human needs.

The key to making this work is properly putting yourself in your prospects shoes; remember Pete the proverbial prospect? This is where you have to master the art of empathy; you need to learn how to feel what Pete feels.

Now let's go back to our travel agency brochures for another example. Let's take Pete the proverbial prospect, and do an exercise with the travel brochures. Pete wants to take his wife on a romantic getaway for his upcoming anniversary and he wants to go on a cruise. Pete is on the sales funnel for this and he's pretty far down the cycle to around 65 or 75. Meaning he's pretty much decided that he wants to take a cruise but he probably won't be buying tickets soon because he's not planning on taking the cruise for several months.

So Pete is checking things out travel wise; he's online looking at Cruise deals, he's asking friends about cruise options and experiences and maybe even looking up some local travel agents for help. What is Peat feeling? He's probably excited, maybe a bit nervous; he's never been on a cruise before and he doesn't know what to expect. He wants to make sure he gets the best deal in terms of value and he doesn't want to have any negative experiences; can you feel what Pete feels? Can you put yourself in his shoes?

Now, Pete runs across these two brochures one says "what in the world would you like to do" and the other says "the five secrets of experienced travellers" so which one do you think Pete is going to pick up, which one seems to offer information that is important and relevant to Pete? Well it's the five secrets brochure it's obvious.

Pete is about to travel and he has many questions about travelling; here's a brochure that promises to let Pete in on some secrets from experienced travellers so naturally he's going to check it out. As long as the brochure does a good job of maintaining emotional connections with such headlines and logically informs him with quality information, that brochure will be in a position to sell Pete something; more than likely to sell it to him sooner than he thought he was going to be ready.

Now you understand the importance of connecting with your prospects. I really think you should pat yourself on the back and here' why; understanding this critical component, the connect component of the Local market domination formula puts you head and shoulders above your competition. While the other agencies are perpetually stuck running lame ads with nauseating clichés, you're going to be on your way towards total market dominance with marketing material that has powerful articulated headlines that snap prospects out of auto mode and into conscious mind using emotionally relevant and important hot buttons; that is awesome.

Chapter 10: Inform

Now that Pete the proverbial prospect has had his attention captured; you have completed step one, which is to emotionally connect; and have completed step two, by identifying his hot buttons the next step is to inform.

You now need to become the source of any and all relevant information in regards to your product or services, and your industry altogether. You must be the fountain from hence all knowledge flows. Offer your prospect enough quality, not necessarily quantity, but enough quality information about what to look for, what to avoid and what constitutes the best deal.

In short, you need to define the criteria for what the very best option in your industry is; not only should you define it, but you should already have innovated yourself to the point where nobody else can offer this. That you are in control the whole time; define what constitutes the best deal and you also happen to be the only company who can deliver on the ideal.

The way to do this is to think like an attorney for a moment, now, don't think like an attorney in terms of mimicking the advertising because attorneys are just about as bad at creating marketing materials as everybody else. In fact attorneys are remarkably bad at creating ads, especially considering what they do for a living.

Think about it as that an attorney's job is to prove a point; guilty or innocent, that's it. They can't use clichés and they must be specific and provide real evidence to convince a jury of 12, without any reasonable measure of doubt.

In marketing it's the same thing; you've got to build a case that brings people to the conclusion that *they'd have to be completely insane to work with anybody else but you, no matter the price.*

Now let's get serious about this education process and talk about a life or death court case. Imagine you're the attorney in a life or death court case; in other words, if you lose, your client the defendant is going to be put on death row; if you win your client will be set free, that is a serious scenario.

How are you going to win; are you going to win by building a case that demonstrates without any measure of doubt the client is innocent, are you going to collect as much evidence as possible, are you going to get expert witnesses, character references, alibis and everything else possible so you have a mountain of a case that essentially proves your client's innocence? Wouldn't you agree that Marketing is like building a case 101? Yet remarkably in advertising nobody does this, not even attorneys; I'll prove it to you.

Here are some headlines from criminal defence attorneys in our local phone book. Remember these are the guys have to defend people who may be on trial for something as serious as murder; if you're an innocent man who has been falsely accused of murder and you could face capital punishment, don't you want an attorney who can properly build a case to defend you?

Of course you do, but here's the ironic thing, even good criminal defence attorneys who do a great job building the case in a court of law, fail when it comes to marketing themselves. Check out these headlines; hard charging criminal defence you need a lawyer who doesn't back down. Please; somebody get out the cliché meter because these lawyers are going down.

I mean come on "hard charging criminal defense"; well I would hope so. "You need a lawyer who doesn't back down"; well "I would hope so"; Again, who else can say that? How about everybody attorney on town, that's who.

The next two ads have lawyers name at the top of the headline and then they have a laundry list of bullet points describing what they do, you know; drug cases, domestic violence, all felonies, misdemeanours DUI etc. Guess what, everybody's list is the same from one ad to the next, they're all the same. I mean it's pitiful; none of them pass the cross out write in test or the other cliché evaluations.

The next ad takes the cake, and yes these are real ads. Check out your phone book and I bet you'll find there are ads nearly identical. Here's the next headline; Experience and Professionalism; Really? Come on, I mean really; Experience and Professionalism. Okay so I've just been falsely accused of murder; my life and my families lives are on the line; I face a potential death sentence if a good attorney does not build a proper case to prove my innocence and the best thing you can come up with to prove to me that you're the best man for the job is to say Experience and Professionalism.

Well I would hope so; you're an attorney for crying out loud. I mean who else can say that? What else would I expect you to say, lazy, apathetic and expensive; of course not. Remember people say great things about themselves in the form of clichés because nobody cares or nobody was paying attention and everyone else is doing it.

Now remarkably, there is a little gem in one single ad in the criminal defence section of the phone book; it's a great headline, the problem is that it's not actually used as a headline it's some really small text that is just part of the ad copy and is not highlighted; plus it's not articulated as well as it could be but it's still a great line.

Let me rewrite it and share it with you now; remember I want you to be Pete again, Pete the proverbial prospect and put yourself in Pete's shoes. You've been falsely accused of a crime and you're being prosecuted by the state; you need the very best attorney and you're looking at ads for attorneys that say experience and professionalism.

Now next to that you find experienced, aggressive and affordable. Next! How about, when you've been arrested everything changes. Next! Then all of a sudden you see this gigantic headline; I have over 90% not guilty ratio against state prosecutors, my success record is unmatched in the state. Can you say, capturing and connecting? You better believe you can! That ad will get Pete's eye; now we've got Pete's undivided attention we need to educate Pete.

Just like a good lawyer would build a case; here's what you need to do in terms of creating the informational content in your marketing. We first have to determine what the relevant and important issues are in three hot button categories, and then you simply provide the prospects with the information necessary for them to feel like they have all the information they need to make the best decision possible, just like an attorney.

When an attorney begins trial he will address the jury and say something like this; Ladies and Gentlemen of the jury, in this trial I will prove to you that Pete is innocent. I'm going to prove to you beyond a reasonable doubt that Pete could not have committed this crime and I'm going to prove it based on the following evidence. I'm going to bring out these three witnesses that will concur that Pete could not have been involved and I will present two expert witnesses that will testify that the things happened in this way, and in a way that Pete could not have accomplished.

You will have no option but to conclude that he is innocent. See you're going to have to know what those important relevant issues are and then gather and present the evidence.

Ultimately if you present your case, your products and services in a compelling and convincing way you will build confidence with your prospects that you offer the best value. You'll also make them feel like they're in control of the decision. Just like the jury draws the conclusion of not guilty, so will your prospects. They feel like they would have to be completely insane to work with anyone else but you, no matter the price.

So let me share the three hot button categories with you; they are benefits, objections and competition. The benefits category refers to hot buttons that describe the real benefits that customers will gain when buying whatever it is you sell, the objections category refers to the objections that people have when considering buying what you sell and competition refers to hot buttons that describe why people should buy from you instead of one of your competitors.

Let me give you an example of what I mean in the real world. I will use the Lasik eye surgery again so when it comes to Lasik eye surgeon; benefits based hot buttons would be things like, being able to see without glasses, having independence, not having to wear contacts anymore, enjoying beautiful sunsets, not crashing into things at night time and any other real benefit people gain from Lasik eye surgery.

Objections based hot buttons refer to the reasons why people don't want to get Lasik we actually already covered that earlier but in the case of Lasik there are only two major objections; fear and price, that's it. So the hot buttons are in the headlines and the informational content would explain the reasons why these objections are invalid; got that. So the informational content should always serve to invalidate people's objections in advance of their ever meeting with you

Lastly competition based hot buttons describe why somebody should get Lasik from one eye doctor over the other. These are the three hot button categories and you really need to create headlines in all three hot button categories like we described earlier. Then you need to follow up with additional informational content to make and the build case, that you are the obvious choice to do business with. You need to explain your case and provide as much evidence as possible.

For example, you should collect as many testimonials as possible, save and provide snapshots of articles or press stories of your company show books you're featured in, awards you've received, charts and graphs that illustrate your unique selling proposition, client lists or portfolios comparison charts, checklists, earning reports, examples of savings, examples of earnings, expert tests facts and figures, performance audits, photos, videos, product demonstrations, quotes from clients, standards-based checklists, statistics, technical drawings et cetera. Do you get the picture yet? You need to build your case.

Let me give you another quick example; Let's look at a *mythical company* who sells an amazing product for the agricultural industry has called "Super Grow". Now in the AG industry most farmers have been using NPK-based fertiliser on their farms for decades. NPK stands for nitrogen, phosphorus and potassium; but the problem is that this fertilizer serves to feed the crop all the while the soil has been neglected, literally for decades.

The soil itself is a living organism and most farmers have soil that is literally dying and in some cases nearly dead. The result is that the less and less nutrients are able to get into the crops because the soil doesn't have the necessary biological activity to properly transfer nutrients into our crops.

This is one of the major reasons why our food supply has less than nutrition availability than it did when our parents were kids. Anyhow, this client's product Super Grow serves to feed the soil and increases biological activity in the soil allowing the soil to more properly transfer nutrients to the crops. It's amazing; it's a burgeoning industry called the biological industry and is just now starting to go main-stream.

Let me describe some of the hot buttons in their industry. After their interviewing dealers it was revealed that the biggest hot button is that people think its snake oil; the AG industry has a long history of companies coming along with some new products that claim to do everything, (same holds true for the Chiropractic industry, probably all industries) even though it was totally useless; farmers bought it before realizing it was worthless and by then the company has disappeared.

Over time farmers became incredibly sceptical of all new products on the market and have just stuck with the same products and programs they've used for years. So the snake oil perception was a major objection based hot button; the benefits were many as I've already described but additionally the result of the products really helped farmers increase their return investment because Super Grow allowed them to use less fertilizer and get superior crops and get better yields at harvest time.

So as part of their complete marketing system they created a sales brochure that the dealers and salespeople used in the field; the sales brochure had this hot button loaded headline: **Three proven ways farmers can significantly increase their return on investment with Super Grow**. Then when you open the brochure up there are three headlines describing those three proven ways. Let me read those headlines and sub headlines for you.

Number one increased yield. Yes, Super Grow really can increase your yields and we've got the data to prove it. See the informational content below that shares how Super Grow has been able to increase yield all over the world for farmers. It includes graphs and data and describes how Super Grow has had more university testing than any other product of its kind in the world.

It points people to their website where they can access the actual university test results themselves. It also invalidates the common objection, that farmers believe that the products might work for farms in Wisconsin and not and in Iowa, it works in California but not in Florida or whatever; it's actually a common objection. The informational content details how Super Grow has been tested with hundreds of fertilizer programs and dozens of crops in over 30 states in five continents and in all soil textures, in wet seasons and drought and the results consistently show an increase in yield. How's that for invalidating the objection.

The second headline says this: To increase fertilizer utilization stop wasting money with ever-increasing fertilizer costs. Beneath this headline is informational content that describes the science behind how Super Grow works, it includes a testimonial from the farmer, a custom graphic detailing how the increased biological activity does a better job of utilising fertiliser. Again the informational content here is building the case based on the customer's hot buttons.

The third headline is: Increased soil and crops quality; Super Grow enhances much more than can be seen on a yield monitor. Now without taking the time to explain what all that means just suffice to say that these terms are hot buttons in the Ag industry.

In the informational content they provide details about how Super Grow makes this happen. There are comparison pictures from fields that have been partially treated with Super Grow; they show what the fields look like with and without Super Grow, along with images of what the crops look like side-by-side that have been treated with Super Grow. The soil results are amazing, think about it; it's the exact same field just one part of the field used Super Grow and the other part didn't; the difference is yield, crop quality and fertilizer utilization. It's unmistakable and almost unbelievable but the evidence is right there for the entire world to see.

To successfully implement a market strategy as I described, you need to build a case for your target market that provides them with all the facts and evidence that they need for them to determine your product or service is the obvious choice. You need to get enough quality information so they feel like *they'd have to be completely insane to work with anyone else but you; no the matter the price.*

Chapter 11: Incentivizing

The next component of the local market domination formula is incentivizing. We talked about this briefly already but the point here is to give your customers a low risk incentive to take the next step in the buying process. In other words you need to move your prospects down the sales funnel and in doing so lead them to you. There's a really important point to make here going back to the concept of the sales funnel. Remember how we talked about how there are always more people who would be considered future buyers, compared to now buyers. The future buyers make up points 1-80 or so in the sales funnel; all the now buyers make up points 80-100.

So here's the beauty of the fourth component, the incentive. This step gives the opportunity to capture the contact information of 100% of the sales funnel; not just now buyers and not just future buyers but everybody. It also puts you in control of your target market and gives you direct access to them without having to rely so heavily on advertising in traditional, orthodox marketing mediums.

Think about it, what would you give to have the contact information for everybody in your target markets that are going to buy what you sell in the next year? If you had such a list what would you send those people? You see how obvious this all starts to become.

So now the question is how do you get that information, and start feeding them targeted information that is relevant and important to them? Well you do so with an incentive; remember you simply need to sell the next step in the buying process. The easiest way to do this is with free or very low cost high value marketing tools that contain information that is relevant and useful to the client. Things like free reports, free videos, free audio training, free lessons, special discounts, urgency based limited offers etc.

Let me give you some examples; let's say you're a home builder and you want to sell some new homes along with all the other home builders in the area, so what do you do? You put together a bunch of ads in the newspaper that are filled with smiling happy people with perfect complexions and perfect white teeth, who are laughing and enjoying themselves in a picturesque home with the headline that says something like; "Love where you live," or "Isn't it time to live in a happy home?" Or some other ridiculously lame cliché like that. I mean that's what you're going to see every home builder on the planet do but its all wrong and you should know that by now.

So what should they do instead? Well they should follow the strategic messaging formula. By now you should at least know that they need to capture their prospects attention and connect with them on an emotional level using hot button loaded headlines and sub-headlines. Then they should provide enough informational content to build a legitimate case as to why their homes are the superior option; then they should provide an incentive to take the next step in the buying process.

This is actually a great example because how many people in any given market want to buy a home right now? Imperatively speaking, very few compared to the number of people who are going to one day buy a home in any given market. The numbers who are going to buy a home right away is pretty small. But nearly all advertising only goes after those who are in the market to buy now.

Who else would those ridiculously common cliché based ads I just described appeal to; only people who want to buy a house now. They see an ad for new homes, they want to buy a new home right away so they say to themselves hey, let's check it out. There's no real reason why they should buy it from one homebuilder over another.

However if a builder followed the strategic marketing formula and then gave prospects an incredible incentive he could then capture the information of the target market and control their movement along the sales funnel, facilitating the decision making process and eventually lead prospects to their front door.

Let me give you an example of how to do this. The first and one of the easiest is with a special report, here's some titles for a special report; "Seven home builder secrets you must know before buying a new home," or "How to get the best deal on a new home without getting burned," or "Home buying success strategies, how to buy a new home with no money down, with free upgrades and without any hassle." I could go on and on with sample headlines but any of these would work.

Then you provide this free report as an offer in your ad, after you've captured, connected and informed; now you incentivise with an offer like this "Go to freehomereport.com to download your free copy of the special report seven home builder secrets you must know before buying a new home."

You see, it's a low risk offer that give prospects a simple incentive to take the next step in the buying process. Then when they get to your website you ask them enter their name and email address and click submit to get their free report instantly and automatically; then BAMM! You have their contact info.

In the world of internet marketing we call this an opt-in; you see if the prospect has not opted in to your list you are not positioned to sell them your products or services at a later time because you are not in control of the information they receive about you industry or about you for that matter from that point on.

Another great offer is a series of videos, nowadays people love videos, especially short web-based videos like people are accustomed to seeing on YouTube, in fact the seven home builder secrets report we just mentioned could be turned into a series of videos that prospects get access to in the same method just described. The offer would be re-written to say, "Get immediate access to 7 free videos describing 7 home builder secrets you must know before buying a new home.

I think you get the picture by now; you can use this technique in nearly any industry, we've used it successfully by offering free DVD's, free reports, free tickets to live events, immediate coupons and more. Coupons are actually a very simple and obvious way to build your list especially for local service based businesses.

You may already offer a coupon for something right, you might even be paying money to a mailing program like Valpak or some other coupon vendor; but my suggestion is to put an opt in form on your website and offer visitors a valuable coupon in exchange for their contact information.

Just remember when you're creating incentives for your prospects; make sure the incentive is low risk, if a prospect reads the offer you are making to them and it immediately causes them to think or feel like they're going to get hammered with a sales call or some other high pressured sales experience they're going to avoid your incentive like the Plague. Just make it low risk and make sure it has legitimate value.

Chapter 12: Automate

So here's a relevant point to be made, follow up sequences need to be automated. As humans we are terrible about following up, we always forget or come up with excuses but today there are hundreds of automatic follow up tools that can do this for you even if you don't use an automated piece of software you should still create a specified follow up system or sequence that is manually executed in the exact same manner every time for every customer as part of your overall marketing system. No matter what you do just make sure that every prospect is followed up with multiple times with high quality relevant information that captures, connects, informs and yes incentivizes.

Now automatic follow up is nothing new, right. Everybody has seen auto responders in their emails but the point I'm making in the local market domination formula is you need to ensure that the content in your follow-up is important and relevant to the customer. That's why I just mentioned the fact that you need to use the first 4 components of the local market domination formula in your automatic follow up process.

Here's why, if you bombard your target market with a bunch of automatic sales messages that they don't care about they'll end up hating your guts because they'll think you're annoying. However, if they get high quality information from you that is important and relevant based on emotional hot buttons they'll start to look forward to the stuff you send them. They'll say to themselves, perhaps even subconsciously, everything I get from this company is great stuff, whether it comes in the mail, email or any other follow up method... people will love you if you send the right information. This just builds more confidence and allows you to gain control of your prospects journey down the sales funnel ultimately leading them to buy from you!

The numbers of examples here again is endless, but let's use another real life example with an ad company I mentioned earlier. One of the ways they meet new prospects is at trade shows for the ad industry, so we put together an automatic follow up system using a piece of software that automatically follows up with customers via text, voice mail and email; it's pretty slick.

Here's how it works; when a sales associate meets a prospect at a trade show they do what everybody else does, and gets their business card. Now a business card is an amazing tool because it has the prospects contact information on it, like I mentioned earlier sales people usually never follow up. Most sales people have huge stacks of business cards of people they've never followed up with; not these sales people because their armed with an automatic follow up system. This is the fifth component of the local market domination formula so you've got to do it.

So let's call our sales person Billy; what Billy does is simple, every time he gets a business card from someone he takes out his smartphone and scans their card using a custom app, the app then automatically transcribes the contact information and puts the prospect into an automated follow up campaign.

In this case there are actually 7 ways to get someone's contact information on the list using our software; including texting the information, sending an email, calling in to a custom phone number, scanning a QR code, filling in a form on a website or manually inputting the information into the software, or of course using the smart phone app. However, at a trade show where business cards are being exchanged, using the smart phone app is the easiest method.

So here's what happens automatically after the card is scanned. Within minutes the contact information is transcribed and the prospects information is in the software system, the software then sends out a direct to voicemail voice message, in other words the client's cell phone never rings, it just indicates that they have a voicemail.

When the prospect listens to the voicemail they hear a message from Billy that says this, "Hi, this is Billy from Super Grow Industries, it was nice meeting you earlier today at the trade show. I just want to let you know that I sent you an email with my contact information so you don't lose it. I'll follow up with you next week, take care.

"Simple and harmless right but it makes a big impact with the prospects. Then within minutes they get a text message from Billy that says "This is Billy from Super Grow Industries, it was nice meeting you at the trade show, and I just sent you an email." The system also automatically sends out that email that says this, "Hello first name, and of course first name would be the prospects actual first name. It was nice meeting you at the trade show today, I just wanted to let you know that I will follow up with you next week so I can share some case studies with you and you can see how Super Grow has helped increase our customers ROI in at least 3 different ways. I know you'll find the information valuable; also my contact information is below.

"Pretty strong right, the software automatically touches the prospect 3 times in a low key way, this method is non-offensive and it makes prospects fell like you're diligent and hard working as opposed to pesky and annoying.

Then three days later the system automatically sends an email with the headline that says, 3 ways to increase ROI, the email then says "Hi first name, this is Billy from Super Grow Industries, we met last week at the trade show. As promised I am sending you a link that describes three ways that our customers are increasing their ROI using Super Grow; you can learn these methods here.

Now there's a link to their website with the specific content mentioned. You see how the email is short, to the point and how it facilitates the decision making process based on relevant hot buttons?

The next email comes six days after they first meet and this email says this in the subject line, the science behind Super Grow, the body content says this. "Hi, first name, we've put together a short video that I know you'll find valuable since so many products today simply have no real science behind their claims, Super Grow is different. The video is aptly titled the science behind Super Grow, once you understand it you'll use it guaranteed, you can watch the video here.

They click the link and can instantly watch this video which is a super high production video with animations, graphics, testimonials and scientific explanations that describe how their product works and what type of results farmers are getting. Yes the video was expensive to produce but it's powerful and it works. Remember if you want to dominate you have to do what it takes.

Then after 9 days, the get another email with the headline that says, where should I send this report. The email then says this, "Hi first name, I was reviewing this new special report that we just printed and I thought of you, it's titled 3 proven ways farmers can significantly increase their return on investment with Super Grow, there's some great detail about soil microbiology that most farmers are completely unaware of along with lots of data and evidence. I would love to send you a copy of it, what address should I send it to?

This email is awesome because it requests interaction, also do you see how this follow up sequence is following the strategic messaging formula, the previous emails were connecting and informing and now we're incentivizing. Here's the deal, not everyone's going to respond to this email, we understand that but those who do are going to be hot leads and of course all of this is done with zero effort on your part since the software handles it for you.

I'm not going to take the time to review the rest of the follow up sequence in detail but in short the additional emails go out and offer informational content based on the target markets hot buttons. It includes links to more videos, testimonials and evidence. There's also an offer to receive a free DVD.

The last message is actually a text message that simply says "This is Billy from Super Grow industries, what day is a good day to call you? After 9 automatic contacts in less than 30 days with the tremendous amount of value included in those contacts it's simply human nature to respond and when the prospect responds to his text message the text is automatically forwarded to Billy's email so he knows that the prospect responded and then he can follow up accordingly.

As I'm sure you can see automatic follow up is a powerful new weapon in any companies marketing arsenal, I think you'd have to be crazy not to implement this kind of a tool. We use it in our own business and we use it for our clients. Can you see yourself using an automatic follow up system like this? What kind of effect do you imagine it would have on sales in just this year alone? Think about that as we move on.

Chapter 13: Internet Suite

So now we've covered the first two steps in the Total Domination System. Step 1 is to create or at least highlight some business innovations. Step 2 is to utilize local market domination formula which we just covered in relative detail. The next step, step 3 is to implement a comprehensive internet marketing suite.

I'm not really going to spend much time on this because the content here's quite voluminous and it doesn't make for good training content because it's based on techniques and strategies, and it involves internet technology, software, special tips and all sorts of other granular details that become a bit overwhelming to have to read and understand.

In short the purpose of point 3 in the Total Domination System is to develop and automate an online marketing program that serves as the backbone for your overall marketing system. This includes building a website that is used as a marketing tool that actually has a sales and marketing function as opposed to just being an online brochure. We also ensure that for those companies where it's irrelevant that you have an effective social media presence and an online video presence where your company's videos are all featured on your own YouTube channel.

We'll teach you search engine optimization techniques that actually work and that can help you get found on the internet by your prospects that are searching for you. We'll help you develop online omnipresence; many companies talk about your online presence but we encourage you to have online omnipresence, as well as a five star reputation, when your prospects begin investigating your company. The difference is that we are suggesting that as much as is possible you need to be everywhere online at the same time. You can't afford to be missing from anywhere online that your prospects might be.

This is all industry dependent but some examples of places you need to be is on Facebook, Twitter, Yelp, Google+, Yahoo and Bing Local; dozens of other online Yellow pages or local citations based websites, YouTube, Pinterest, Instagram etc. The list is never ending and it grows and changes constantly.

However there is one place that most everybody needs to be on and that's YouTube; this is because nearly all businesses have use for effective marketing videos and YouTube allows you to put your marketing videos in front of the world for free; it's an amazing tool.

Plus when you work with a Local Market Fusion consultant, your consultant can help you get your YouTube videos ranking at the top of nearly any search for the keywords relevant to your business.

We have a near 100% success rate in doing so even for incredibly competitive search terms and guess what YouTube is now the number 2 search engine on the internet. In other words, after Google the most common place people search for something online is YouTube, even more than

Yahoo and Bing. So you really can't afford to NOT be on YouTube.

Again the strategies here are too numerous to explain but you can get more details about this part of our program on the Local Market Fusion website at LocalMarketFusion.com.

So in short when it comes to the internet you need to be everywhere all at once and you need to make sure your website is utilized as a tool in your overall market

Chapter 14: Systematized Sales Process

Step four in the Local Market Domination system is to create and implement systamatized sales process. This is one of the most overlooked aspects of a complete marketing system but those who utilize it will increase sales and maximise efficiencies, while simultaneously driving revenue and lowering costs.

Sounds good right, I mean it almost sounds too good to be true, but it's not, it's just the guaranteed results that come from hard work done right. A lot of what we do here comes from my experience of developing and operating multiple Chiropractic Clinics, as well as coaching hundreds of solo practitioners, as well as Entrepreneurs in business. I found to have a growing company requires a system.

Early To Bed Early To Rise Work Like Hell and Systematize!

When you operate in a system and then come to a business that is not closely following a proven approach it becomes quickly apparent why most businesses fail. That reason is that most small business owners are experts at their trade or craft but they're not experts at running a business, it's a big difference and it's the difference that makes the difference.

My solution to the problem is to create and implement systems in your business to do the heavy lifting for you, so that your business is a streamlined and nearly automated machine that makes money for you without the need for constant and perpetual oversight. That's the oversimplified explanation of what the book is about, so we've created this step in the Local Market Domination system, to ensure that your entire sales and marketing program system process is systamatized we don't want to leave anything to chance; especially considering how much work is involved in creating marketing programs.

For customers it's an important analogy; think about how much effort and infrastructure goes into creating a newspaper. I know, newspapers are dying and will be extinct in a generation but just go with me for a minute.

In order to produce just one newspaper the publisher has to employ a small army of people to gather news information, write news articles, edit them, typeset the content, layout the paper, design the ads, sell the ads and then actually have printing presses and press operators in place to run overnight while we sleep so that the most recent news is available to us in the morning.

It's an incredible amount of effort and infrastructure all designed to get you to read the paper but after all the effort that goes into just one paper the paperboy takes the paper and throws it in the mud.

So then will the prospect even read the paper? No he won't, all the effort and infrastructure developed by the publisher is ruined in one split second when the paperboy throws it in the mud.

The same goes for your business... no matter how much effort you put into creating the most incredible business in your industry and how well articulated your marketing and advertising is; it can all be ruined in a split second during the sales process. If your sales people don't have a systamatized sales process to follow they could throw your company in the mud at the last minute right before your products or services are properly delivered to your prospects.

The way to overcome this is with a complete systamatized sales process.

The 5 step Process to Acquire New Clients
Acquiring, Connecting and Transforming Suspects into Clients.
"The Practice Ignition system"

Suspects to clients: As a Chiropractor I found those that don't know you are referred to as "The Cold Market", and are suspicious at best as to how your service actually benefits them... They just don't understand the true value of your service, there for they are considered the "cold "market.

Since they don't really know or understand the service you offer, they don't know if it is the best choice for them, so they ask others, who most often don't know either and they base their decision on hearsay.

Based on that it became incredibly obvious that advertising my product, and by the quality of the clients I was attracting through advertising , that advertising for a unique service is a total waste of time if your goal is to build a practice or business that is based upon a certain culture.

In chiropractic the culture I represented was that of living a vital and healthy life, free of interference in the nervous system either by chemical, mental or structural involvement. This philosophy is becoming known in the alternative health world but hardly understood in the market place for those seeking the benefit Chiropractic care offers.

The populations I see attracted to Chiropractors through advertising are those seeking quick pain relief, of which those services are covered by health insurance. In other words, advertising attracts those looking for the allopathic approach to health which is sick care and not the Chiropractic approach which is to restore health, rather than mask a symptom temporarily as is the practice of medicine.

So the truth seems to be that those who seek chiropractors are coming for reasons that are not the unique approach to health offered by the Chiropractor.

This may be a contributing reason why Chiropractors seem to be in constant search for new clients. The following is a system which is designed to promote the unique factors of "your business service" and to attract those looking for that benefit who may not even know you provide that service.

This obvious disconnect is a great example and an argument for why advertising may not work for your particular service, because of the lack of understanding to the cold market of your service benefits, and why the formation of a true marketing program may be the answer to vastly increase your present market efforts.

The challenge with advertising is that you are marketing to people that do not know, like or trust you, and most always don't really understand what the true value of your service is…

Because of this… they search you out as a common commodity shopping by price and convenience. With little attention to your unique and valuable benefit, comparing you to others who may not have the skills you possess, which is the genesis of the phrase, "comparing apples to oranges.

It is hard to market to a population totally ignorant to your unique benefit and value; these are reasons this author has been often heard as saying advertising a misunderstood service will only work when associated to a common problem, yet may not attract the clients who desperately need your service.

That comment can be proven by the number of people who arrive at a business yet fail to return; they didn't see the value for themselves, and the proprietor or doctor failed to demonstrate how the service could and would provide what they were seeking.

It is hard to operate a business when your benefit is not known or misunderstood and miss-judged and evaluated on the merits of another service that "they" compare it to, yet has no real connection with.

Magnetic marketing is the process of drawing the market to you for the reasons they seek, not for what they may or may not know about it.

The Lead Magnet: Step one is creating the magnet.

This lead magnet is designed to provide an irresistible bribe that hits your target market right between the eyes and compels them to give their contact information in exchange for the promised bribe.

This is important because when the lead provides the contact information they have agreed to let you send information to them and because of this they will assuredly read what you send.

This is how we begin to communicate the value and benefit of our product or service. Since the lead magnet is typically the start of the marketing funnel, it is also usually the highest point of leverage.

At this writing in February 2014 I have heard seasoned marketers state that at this time after the last economic turmoil it is the hardest time ever to get the first dollar or the first "sign" that someone is willing to be marketed to. But it is not the hardest time to get sales after they have agreed to begin the process.

Lead magnets are good because your suspects want immediate gratification and something they can sink their teeth into as they search for solutions NOW. Lead magnets give them that.

A lead magnet can be a Free report, a webinar or public talk, (I like the idea of dinner banquets, this was my foundational approach in developing my 13 Chiropractic clinics).

Finding what they are looking for is like a mouse finding their cheese. It has been said a mouse will chew through steel if they know there is cheese on the other side.

Therefor it is the entrepreneur's "duty" to know their avatars (client profile) cheese (needs and wants), and promote that as you would chees to a mouse. If they perceive you have what they want you have their attention, you could say they are now your client to lose, if they don't see or perceive you do have what they need and want. (This explains potential clients coming to your place of business telling you what they need and then don't come back) they didn't see their cheese at your office.

One famous lead magnet was from a person marketing a dating service, his lead magnet was, the "kiss test". A lesson in how to know if she is ready to kiss you, everybody seemed to want to know that test and it was very successful as a bribe, giving him permission to market his program to those accepting that bribe.

What do you have to offer a suspect which has a high perceived value and would be wanted by those seeking the benefits you offer, that could use your service? Well give it a way! It is way better than a business card that gets lost or thrown away and is totally irrelevant in providing your benefit!

"But my book has value and I would like to sell it" you say! Imagine if you received something of great perceived value that helped you in a situation, how would you feel about the person who gave it to you Great: right? How do you feel you would think about that person if they presented an offer to purchase something from them? You might just feel that after reading their incredible little book this person gave you, Wow!

this person gave me that great little book for FREE, it was so awesome; this product must be incredible if he is selling it!

Do you see the advantage of the "Lead Magnet" Now?

Step Two has been referred to as **"The Trip Wire"**. As a person begins the journey on your sales funnel, your first goal is to ask for a sale... Of something! Actually it should be a product of high perceived value that goes along with the upcoming "Core Offer" you will be presenting.

In developing my practices I use a dinner banquet as a lead magnet, promising great information to improve your health and vitality... and I feed them as well! People love to be fed!

The close of that program... is actually a trip wire. In the beginning I would offer a free evaluation in the clinic to see if they could be helped. I would get a fair amount of the audience to sign up, and less than half would actually show. I actually violated what I later found as necessary to close an audience, which I refer to as the tripwire!

When people would accept my free offer then not show I decided they were just flakes, and didn't get it. Knowing what I now know I didn't give enough perceived value for the offer, or ask for a commitment of any kind on their part, which is money. They didn't feel the value of the offer and chose to not come. It wasn't even worth their time to investigate.

Now I offer a high value 4 day pass to my practice that includes my giving them vital information to make a decision to become a client and also gives me information as to their need. I go into detail at the end of the talk as to the value and benefit of the service they will receive and explain It is a service that most doctors would charge over $450 dollars for. I sell them the trip wire offer for only $47 bucks. Now almost 100% show up... That small transaction has actually transformed the suspect from a seeker to a buyer.

The name trip wire was coined by a man named Perry Belcher, of Digital Market LLC. He is known for his "Secret Selling" techniques and as a result of studying under him I have applied a few of his strategies for use in my market to promote my service's which is the opposite of his business of selling physical products.

The trip wire is an irresistible, super – low – ticket offer that converts prospects into buyers. The psychology of the trip wire is, once a customer takes their wallet out, they are far more likely to leave it out and continue spending money with your company... and the most valuable to you is they just transitioned from a suspect to a buying customer. They have made a buying transaction, they have belief in you and they have switched from that of a cold market suspect, who doesn't know or trust you to an informed client of your service that now knows and trusts you, demonstrated by the fact they gave you money... even a small amount represents that transition.

The Dopamine Effect

Perry Belcher did some research on why the trip wire works. Why does spending some money will drive a person to want to spend more?

The findings were that when a person makes a purchase they get a release of dopamine in the brain and it makes them feel good. Ever hear of a person saying, "I need retail therapy"? Have you ever felt bad about something and found yourself shopping? Then walking out of the mall loaded with shopping bags and a whole lot of new credit card debt, yet feel great!

Yes it feels good mentally to buy, and when people are allowed to buy they feel good about you as well. Look at how many shoppers defend their stores as being the best store; or product! My favorite story is what I call the "Kirby Vacuum" effect.

Have you ever known anyone who bought a Kirby? I have... One night while having a few friends over, a plant got knocked over. I went to get my vacuum and when I walked in with my everyday Hoover, this guy jumped up. "I'll go and get my Kirby", he stated, as if he was going to save the day.

I said no problem this will be fine and he jumped in and began to tear down any vacuum other than a Kirby to shreds, he almost sounded as if he was going to have all vacuums banned if not a Kirby. He even said we should test his theory by having a "suck challenge" to determine whose vacuum sucked the hardest and could suck the most dirt!

I found this so funny! Yet it wasn't until a few years later that I understood. He had paid about 3 grand for the Kirby and I paid like 150 bucks for the Hoover. He was invested in the Kirby and had to defend its honor by proving (in his mind) it was the best item. We get attached to things we invest in.

Another story I heard of the trip wire effect was when a man received the most expensive Big Bertha golf club as a gift. He looked at it, and it was a work of art, beautiful! He went home to put the Big Bertha to rest with his other golf clubs and he said that is pathetic... My clubs make the BB look bad!

So off to the golf shop where he bought a new $2,000 set of clubs, a new bag and a new golf wardrobe, spending almost 4 thousand dollars! All because of the new Big Bertha that gave him a good feeling of having new stuff... he spent 4 thousand more, and he didn't really even golf! More than one or two times a year, but now he loves it when he pulls out the new stuff!

The Big Bertha was a trip wire and opened up his wallet even though he didn't pay anything for the Big Bertha, the dopamine effect took place because of the new item!

Are you aware of the new trend of dollar stores? I was told they are successful because people can so much stuff... need it or not 20 items for only 20 bucks! Again getting a lot of new stuff satisfies the brain! People love to shop, get stuff and spend money. Who are we to deny them?

Show your benefit and value and they will come and spend!

Do you ever catch yourself going on a spending spree on yourself after shopping for a gift for someone else? Yes that is the trip wire effect; now let's offer that to your prospects so they can feel good in your business as well.

That is what the trip wire is all about. It is the opposite of those who market their business with free offers, feeling that a lack of risk will attract more clients...

While offering a free item and limiting risk to show your value and benefit is smart and correct as a lead magnet, free only will attract, it just doesn't have a good stick factor.

Those that enter with no risk, and receive service with no monetary exchange will cause the new proposed client to feel being "sold to" when you eventually make an offer.

Because the psychological sales process was not adhered to they become suspicious of why you are not charging (everyone knows there is no free lunch, they are just waiting for the hammer to drop), and may begin to wonder what you're going to drop on them later, become critical of the services and not embrace them because of the fact that by having what I call, no "skin I the game" or have not contributed any money, has caused them to be out of exchange with the business, and become suspicious of it and want to get away from it, before they feel like they owe you something!

Have you ever owed any money to someone and found yourself rationalizing why you shouldn't have to pay them? Usually the longer you owe the more of a jerk the person becomes (in your mind) and the less deserving. This factor also happens in business. So no matter the small size of the trip wire sale, the key is, a monetary transaction must be processed, even if it was only 1 dollar.

The CORE offer

The Core Offer is the flagship product or service that your company is ultimately trying to sell. This is what you are known for, and this is where most of your time and energy is focused.

As a consultant I like to feel my role is more of an optimization partner, where we work together to optimize the conversion rate of your core offer (in health care it is your initial recommendation) so you get better acceptance or conversion rates, from those you have been marketing to.

Imagine your business or practice if you converted every new client to the initial recommendation, what would happen to your retention rates, your income and professional satisfaction, not to mention referrals? The practice would sky rocket, because the people who were investing in your service had a better feeling about you with higher trust and because of your service they actually felt better as well!

The Profit Maximizer

Whether it's an upsell (offering something more of what they already bought) a cross-sell (offering them a related product or service) or a subscription or access to a community or club, every offer needs something on the back end to increase immediate average customer value and overall engagement with the buyer; Because while a buyer is good, a multi-buyer is even better.

Would you like fries and a shake with that? Did you know that McDonalds spends all the profits on a hamburger to get you in the driveway, their profits are exclusively from upsells?

Return Path

Because of the lead magnet offer, we now have the ability to go back to non-buyers and put them into a follow up series to increase initial conversations and future conversions. Maybe they were just not a now buyer and are a future buyer, again follow up will turn old no's into tomorrow's cash!

Equally important, we also have the ability to go back to our buyers who didn't purchase everything in the sales funnel (i.e. trip wire, core offer and profit maximizer) to increase the average customer value.

This is simply having a proven on-going campaign in your "bag of tricks" that you can deploy to generate additional revenue from the traffic and leads you're already receiving.

Chapter 15:
An Example of the System Working

Let me walk you through a case study of a contact so you can see what this would look like. As I mentioned earlier regarding a client who is a local contractor selling heating and air conditioning systems and repair otherwise known as HVAC; that stands for heating, ventilation and air conditioning.

Before being introduced to the Local Market Domination system that client was using all the typical clichés that every other contractor was using, you know been in business since in 1776, same day service, licence bonded and insured and all the rest of that junk; so the perception was that he was "just like everybody else".

However the reality is that they were unquestionably the most innovative company in the industry so innovative in fact he didn't have to create a new innovation, but simply innovated the way he described his unique selling proposition to the marketplace.

The client, we'll call him Jim built his business Express Heating and cooling to be the best in the industry he didn't need any help but Jim's marketing suffered because he wasn't using the Local Market Domination System.

Let me describe the entire marketing system for you, first of all there were dozens of headlines created with different offers and different mediums. They started with the Internet and Yellow Pages because contractors are one of the few industries where prospects still do look people up in the phone book. An online presence was created so the contractor was everywhere, he has a custom designed Face Book page, Google plus page, Twitter accounts and YouTube channel where there are new updates posted every week on all of the social media accounts .

His YouTube channel has over 20 videos related to his industry and his videos dominate the search results for any of his relevant search phrases in YouTube. Because of the local business listing optimization and SEO techniques, his website shows up on one page 1 on most keywords. In fact his number one most profitable keyword was showing up three times on page 1 of Google, once under the map section, once under organic listing and once as a video; in short he was dominating.

When visitors get to his website they are greeted with a pop-up video that only plays the very first time you visit and never again, the video is from the owner himself who thanks visitors for coming and then offers them an immediate discount on a repair by filling out the form on the website.

In his industry there is a lot of skepticism so he had a very advanced testimonial section developed; (a standard service by Local Market fusion for marketing your reputation). So when you click on the testimonial page there were three sets of testimonials. The first actual audio recordings of phone calls from customers who have called in and given testimonials while speaking with customer service... there were dozens of them. Below that there are video testimonials from customers who share their positive experiences then beneath that well over 1000 signed testimonials in PDF format with customers raving about their experience with Express Heating and Cooling and they're all conveniently arranged by ZIP Code; so can click on your ZIP Code and find testimonials from dozens of your neighbours.

They also had created another pop-up video on the testimonial page with the owner Jim describing the testimonial page, proudly proclaiming on this page you'll find more testimonials then you're probably ever seen in your life and you know what... its true!

Have you ever been to a website with over 1000 testimonials and three formats on one page for a local contractor, or for any industry for that matter? I didn't think so, you see they were serious about people knowing them and knowing they were the best, they were seeking total dominance for their service in their service community.

In the Yellow Pages they had a double track ad with a full page dedicated to service and repairs and the other full page dedicated to new sales. The service or repair side had a headline that said "we are the only company in California that offers all of this "then there is a list eight features that no other company offers, some of the highlights were; money back service guarantee, if you're not satisfied with the service you receive you get your money back. Nobody offers that, lots of companies offer satisfaction guarantees but not money back guarantees satisfaction guarantee essentially means nothing because it is so subjective.

So you're not satisfied then what; the same company that made you dissatisfied sends another out to do it again; how lame is that. In my case if you're dissatisfied for any reason you get your money back, how is that!

With the confidence based on that one guarantee alone; which heating and air company would you want to use, the one who proudly proclaims to be licensed and bonded and insured or the one who says hey if you are not satisfied with our work will give you 100% of your money back; oh and by the way here's over 1000 testimonials including several dozen neighbours describing their experience with them.

This is what I call a no-brainer; another unique selling proposition is the code of ethics that I described earlier in this program and that same day service. The same-day service implies that many companies offer same-day service, but they really don't provide it and that's the reality of the industry, most companies who offer same-day service usually can't provide it especially in peak seasons like winter and summer.

The full page dedicated to sales of new systems has a headline that states "five secrets contractors don't want you to know", it then goes on to describe how you probably need a new furnace if yours is over 11 years old and what five things you need to know before you make an investment in a new system. We then make an offer to go to a their website to watch their free series of energy-saving videos and to download the free report entitled "the homeowner's guide to hiring service contractors; how to make sure you never suffer by hiring the wrong company" this special report has proved to be one of the most valuable tools in their arsenal.

In it we describe the most common problems that people have with service contractors and how to avoid them; of course the only company that ensures the clients avoid these problems is their company, "Express Heating and Cooling" and of course the report does a great job of highlighting the unique selling propositions of the company that nobody else can offer for example; are you aware of the fact that it's actually possible to have a lean put against your home simply because you hired the wrong heating and air conditioning company?

Not only is this true but it actually happens more times than you'd ever want to believe, the reason for this is simple... if the contractor does not pay for their equipment upfront before they install it in your home, the manufacturer of the equipment has the right to put a lean against your house in order to receive payment.

If this happens to you, you will be forced to pay for equipment twice, now the only way to ensure this does not happen to you is to work with a company that is a cash liquid company... meaning that they own every single piece of equipment they install; guess what this company happens to be the only contractor in the state who is a cash liquid company and is literally the only one that can make this kind of claim to protect customers from having a lean put against their home.

The report then gives homeowners this instruction; to protect yourself, ask your contractor if they actually own the equipment they're installing in your house or are they using payment terms with their suppliers?

Do you see how their facilitating the decision-making process by finding the criteria the prospect should look for in a HVAC contractor will make people feel like *they'd have to be insane to work with anybody else but us, no matter the price?*

But wait, there's more, this is going to get better, they also developed a script from this report; yes it's available online to download for free but they've also printed it out in full colour on glossy stock with UV coating... It is as good as the cover of any National Magazine! Seriously, the printed copy is handed to customers when service technicians arrive at their front door and the script is then recited.

Put yourself in the prospects shoes; imagine you are Pete the proverbial prospect or Pete's wife and your air-conditioner is broken; you call this company to come fix it you're already sceptical and nervous and the technician shows up; when he gets to the door he looks clean and professional and then he recites this to you when you open the door.

"Hello Mrs Jones, my name is Jason with Express Heating and Cooling; we understand that a lot of people are sceptical of service contractors like us because of negative experiences people have had in the past, so in order to protect you from any future grief we prepared this homeowner's guide to hiring service contractors.

Once you've read the information in this guide you will be equipped enough to ensure you never have a bad experience with any contract ever again. I want to go ahead and leave you with a copy, it's free." The technician then hands the printed copy of the report to the customer, how do you think that changes the environment?

What happens to the customer's confidence level? It skyrockets! Think about it, do you see why this company gets thousands of testimonials? And what do you think the customer is doing while the technician is working on their broken equipment? Yes, they're reading the special report and having their confidence built even more; in fact they're being convinced that, whether they realize it or not; Express Heating and Cooling is the very best company of its kind and *they made the best decision possible when they chose them*.

Since the report is printed on such nice paper and looks so nice and professional they don't throw it away; it has perceived value, so it now may sit on their coffee table for friends and family to read when they come over and that of course is just one script.

Local Market Fusion will develop a script for your business as well, so you may exemplify excellent customer service, as your representatives can recite when somebody calls for service or when they call enquiring about a new system.

You see, success is planned and all aspects of customer care must be choreographed. I used to script each and every step, but found clients becoming robotic, now we outline what needs to happen at each moment and create a very real and natural customer experience for you.

You just can't leave things to chance, that is a prescription for mediocrity or total failure. What is required to achieve the success you want is a systamatized marketing and sales process and each step which builds on the next!

All businesses need systems in place to ensure this as much as possible, so all customers hear the same story causing their experience during the sales process to be exceptional.

Those messages were custom scripted using the Local market domination formula and there's still a whole lot more to it; we created a brochure for the technicians to leave to generate leads to the sales team, and again we use a strategic messaging service. We also took the content of the brochure and created three different door hangers; the entire system was developed by using the Local market domination formula and all have special offers with unique headlines.

We also created magnets with special offers and stickers with QR codes to place on furnaces and air conditioners; when a QR code is scanned on a smart phone it automatically calls the company and of course, the phone number's there too.

So if and when a customer has a problem with their furnace their number is easy to find, and speaking of smart phones we also developed a mobile website that is optimized for mobile phones with tactical features and other mobile specific content.

There were also over 15 radio created ads using Strategic Messaging and over 30 postcards and sales letters to generate new business especially during spring and fall when the repairs slow down.

Once these come back to the sales team we developed which probably is one of the most advanced sales system in the industry; which encompasses a complete sales presentation with customised graphics and a custom developed sales script, and when I say customised graphics I mean every single page of this sales presentation was custom designed with the clients branding and imaging; it included pictures of poor installations compared with good ones, what to look for, what to avoid including actual pictures of competitors vans and trucks with their company names photo shopped out and replaced with generic names but the customer gets the point.

As your business and marketing consultant Dr. Bruce A. Parker will walk you, the client, through the entire process of what to look for in (the promotion, sales process and fulfillment of your service.

You see every other (company in your niche) will promote their business with the same lazy clichés, and all look alike while your business will stand out and stand alone as the business

Now understand developing a comprehensive system is a major undertaking and there are more details on to create a similar system with every step of the development process, it takes a lot of energy and effort to ensure that were maximising the results every step along the way.

So what was the end result of implementing the systamatized sales process? Well, starting the first week they implemented the sales system the sales presentations went from being an average of three hours long to 45 minutes long; closing ratios were up by over 30% and margins were up by over 11%.

They have doubled the size of the sales force; in fact after one year of implementing the complete marketing program like I just described, the company had to hire 15 new employees; they've had record sales continuously in each quarter, they became the number one company in their industry and are actually the largest contractor in the state; I don't just mean the largest HVAC contractor but the largest contractor period.

They're actually now one of the top 50 HVAC contractors in America, they're about to break eight figures in revenue; which is an amazing feat in their industry. In short in about years' time they have achieved total dominance. Now I know you're probably thinking; yeah those are great results but look at how much work you had to do to get there.

Exactly, that's the point, if you want to be number one, if you want to reach a place of total dominance there are no shortcuts; you have to do the work that I described here.

Our program is not called the wimpy marketing program, the average marketing program or the corporate marketing program, it's called the Local Market Domination system! The reason for this is because it's truly powerful, it works and it really only applies to businesses who have the courage to do the work. In other words, businesses and business owners who are powerful enough to take this information and implement the program can achieve total dominance.

The reason is when you make the effort and make the investments I have described in this book; superior results are inevitable. You can and should absolutely rise to total dominance in your industry, in your market sector.

I've given you several different examples and case studies in this book, all in different industries so you can see how the scientific approach works in all industries. Since it's based on human nature there are no exceptions to this rule, regardless of your industry. No matter what you sell, if you're local or regional or national or international, if you sell to consumers or business to business; as long as you're selling to humans this system will work... period!

Now as you are aware there is a fifth step in the Local Market Domination program; that step is having a professionalized image. For the sake of time, I'm not going to review this step in detail but the point here is simply obvious; if you want to dominate you must always act and look like a professional.

A professional image directly impacts the amount of confidence your prospect has in you, and remember what you learned earlier; the amount of money someone is willing to give you is directly proportional to the amount of confidence they have in your ability to provide them with the goods and services that they want or need. So just remember in everything you do, look like a professional, act like a professional and be a professional; the market deserves it, so consider it your duty.

Chapter 16: Summary

I hope you enjoyed what you read in this book; I have covered a lot with you. We talked about the two most common marketing mistakes that businesses are making; we talked about eliminating clichés and implementing a complete marketing system.

We also discussed the importance of business innovation, and discussed in relative detail about how the local market domination formula can allow you to craft messages that cut through a cluttered marketplace and cause your prospects and customers to draw the conclusion; that they'd have to be completely insane to work with anybody else but you, no matter the price.

I also gave you plenty of examples and case studies along the way, but here's the shocking part. Believe it or not what you've learned is literally just the tip of the iceberg; implementing the complete Local Market Domination system in its entirety covers every facet of a company's marketing plan.

To find out more you're going to have to connect with me and/or attend one of my webinars. To connect with me please visit www.LocalMarketFusion.com and request a totally FREE marketing analysis, where you will discover how your business presence ranks against your closest competitors.

Again this is a totally FREE service and I guarantee you will learn a lot about your market presence as well as your competitor, which will give you an unfair advantage over them.

Thank you so much for taking the time to learn about marketing and advertising in this book. I am certain and confident that you've learned plenty about marketing your business properly. I hope you can understand now, why we have titled the system "Local Market Domination"; and how to become the number one company in your industry using this system.

The good news is that now you've learned what it takes to do marketing the right way; the bad news is that for most people, even though they learn how to change their marketing by following this program; they often don't do it.

There are typically one of two reasons they give; one is because the old way, the wrong way of doing marketing is so ingrained on their minds that they simply can't get out of that mode of thinking and they're unable to execute the Local Market Domination System...Old habits die hard.

Number two, believe it or not, some people become hurt and offended that you've not only told them that they've done something wrong, but proved it and demonstrated it through our various evaluations that we've shown in this book, that they simply won't change; to do so would be to admit error. My question for those is: *"Do you want to be rich or right"?*

I know that sounds ridiculous, but I'm telling you that people's egos are so fragile that they would rather stay with what is not working, lose money and destroy their companies profit potential, rather than admit that they have been doing marketing wrong. It's just another facet of human nature.

As a business coach I am faced with this daily and it has proven to be very difficult. I had one client tell me that I was her coach and it was my duty to do what she wanted... Even when I had shown her systems were wrong and totally ineffective, beg based on emotions and feelings.

To run a real business of 7 figures plus you are required to know who you serve, your avatar client, what they need and what they want, and do it by research their needs and wants not your feelings, of what they should want.

For me I know my clients as Avatars, what they want, and what they are afraid of. In providing a consulting service my job is to get them there, and sometimes they don't like it, like a child may not like spinach! This is one time when the customer may not be right, and when it becomes necessary to go against a client's wishes when the wishes are not in the clients best interest.

The decisions based on "it should work", or "it is what we have always done" are wrong and based on emotion. I have said more than a thousand times that emotions are for the bedroom, while facts logic and proven strategies are for the boardroom.

Sometimes however, in order to helped a client I have to give them a healthy dose of the truth, and in marketing the truth will set your profits free. Think about it; if we can increase your company's profits from 5 to 5000%, wouldn't you consider that helpful, and worth swallowing a little uneducated pride?

What would it mean to you personally if you could double or triple your company's bottom line this year? What would it mean to you personally if you could afford to hire additional employees and provide more income to your existing employees?

How would you feel if you knew that you were the number one company in your niche and your business was the standard by which all others were judged? Think about it, marketing has the potential to bring all those feelings into reality.

I can tell you that the most fulfilling part of my job is going on site to the client's offices and seeing the new employees that they've had to hire since we've been working with them; helping them grow the companies. There's nothing more rewarding than that for me. You're probably wondering what appears next but three main options remain at this point;

1. Perhaps you've learned enough in this book that you won't need any more help and that is entirely possible. If so, fantastic; I'm sure you will consider the purchase of this book money well spent.

2 A highly popular option is to attend a live seminar or webinar with me. They are held online as well as all over the country and even worldwide. You can find one by visiting the LocalMarketFusion.com website to find out dates and times.

3. Lastly, some of you may want to engage Local Market Fusion in a one-to-one consultative relationship for your business. You can do this by again by connecting with me through the Local Market Fusion website. Look for the button that says click here for your free 45 minute strategy session.

Doesn't it make the most sense to have an experienced business consultant and trained marketing executive implement the Local Market Domination system for you to ensure you have maximised your return on investment?

Planning for your success will take place through regular private mastermind sessions and weekly marketing content reviews, when you engage Local Market Fusion and Dr. Bruce Parker as your business marketing strategist.

I will personally review the content being developed for your own marketing system and help in its design, so you get the best results possible.

Additionally, we've developed a program directly for our consulting clients. It becomes your virtual marketing department; the concept is simple, in short you'd simply be outsourcing your marketing needs to Local Market Fusion after a custom marketing strategy is created for your local market domination, at a fraction of what it would cost to hire a marketing director, that is not trained in our cutting edge marketing strategy and who more than likely will adopt the old Madison avenue approach to your business which is the old expensive and ineffective way to dominate and own your local market, as you have learned in this book.

When you engage Local Market Fusion to create your own Local Market domination strategy, Dr Parker would work with you privately and you would pay Local Market Fusion a monthly retainer fee, like you would to a lawyer, based on your business growth goal. The specific fees will be determined after an initial consultation; as we discussed in the opening part of this book.

The virtual marketing department is a department dedicated to fulfilling your strategies, and creating your credibility products, like free reports, e-books, websites, informational videos, info graphics, along with your automatic client follow up system.

I must highlight the fact that I am not looking to work with every business in existence... in fact I can actually only offer the virtual marketing department service to one company in an industry in the same market... It will either be you or your competitor; whoever gets to me first.

I am looking to work with a business that really must be the best, which possess such a passion for their customers and doing things the right way that they'll do whatever it takes to get good enough to deserve all the business.

I'm looking for people who can't stomach the thought of a customer doing business with their competitor. If you strive for that kind of excellence then reach out to me today and let us legitimately take your business to the next level.

I want to thank you again for investing your time in reading this book; I wish you health and prosperity in your life and business.

Be your best!

Dr. Bruce Parker CEO
"Local Market Fusion"

PS. Thank you for reading this book, I hope it helps put the marketing process in perspective for you.

As a bonus from me to you, I would like to offer you a totally complimentary 45 minute marketing strategy session, to review any part of your present marketing, or to even create a new funnel for you; whatever will best help you.

To receive the session please email me with the subject line message [*Triple your business Free Strategy Session*]to localMarketFusion1@gmail.com,. and I will follow up with you to schedule. In the meantime, happy marketing! This session is valued at over $500 so this is a "do not miss appointment". It may save you even more in costly ineffective marketing as well!

Always Be Your Best!

Dr Bruce

www.ingramcontent.com/pod-product-compliance
Lightning Source LLC
Chambersburg PA
CBHW051708170526
45167CB00002B/580